# Naked Shameless HUMAN AND FREE

## A Simple Guide to Becoming a Human Being

### IZAERA

**BALBOA.**PRESS
A DIVISION OF HAY HOUSE

Copyright © 2024 Izaera.
Cover image by dcworkartstudio.com

All rights reserved. No part of this book may be used or reproduced by
any means, graphic, electronic, or mechanical, including photocopying,
recording, taping or by any information storage retrieval system
without the written permission of the author except in the case of
brief quotations embodied in critical articles and reviews.

Balboa Press books may be ordered through booksellers or by contacting:

Balboa Press
A Division of Hay House
1663 Liberty Drive
Bloomington, IN 47403
www.balboapress.com
844-682-1282

Because of the dynamic nature of the Internet, any web addresses or
links contained in this book may have changed since publication and
may no longer be valid. The views expressed in this work are solely those
of the author and do not necessarily reflect the views of the publisher,
and the publisher hereby disclaims any responsibility for them.

The author of this book does not dispense medical advice or prescribe the use
of any technique as a form of treatment for physical, emotional, or medical
problems without the advice of a physician, either directly or indirectly. The
intent of the author is only to offer information of a general nature to help
you in your quest for emotional and spiritual well-being. In the event you use
any of the information in this book for yourself, which is your constitutional
right, the author and the publisher assume no responsibility for your actions.

Any people depicted in stock imagery provided by Getty Images are
models, and such images are being used for illustrative purposes only.
Certain stock imagery © Getty Images.

Print information available on the last page.

ISBN: 979-8-7652-4821-8 (sc)
ISBN: 979-8-7652-4823-2 (hc)
ISBN: 979-8-7652-4822-5 (e)

Library of Congress Control Number: 2023923888

Balboa Press rev. date: 01/10/2024

# CONTENTS

# ACKNOWLEDGEMENTS

Where to begin on a life journey? I've had magnificent loves, wonderful parents, and siblings whom I love dearly. I've grown from my relationships, and my gratitude cannot be expressed in words.

The guy that helped to set me free, who befriended me in one of his photography courses—Paul, I miss you. You departed on the next phase of your eternal journey far too soon. Thanks for being here for me and introducing me to all of your friends, who are now my friends.

Stephen, Chris, and Vince, whose presence, comradery, and easy-going humour raised me from the depths of depression—you were there when I needed you most.

Thank you, Kim, my coach, for introducing me to Bob Proctor, who set me free.

Thank you to the team at the Proctor Gallagher Institute for not giving up on me even after I gave up on myself.

Gary and Irina, thank you for accepting me into your lives and supporting me in my out-of-the-box adventures; for teaching me about things I am ignorant of and for your love and patience.

Thank you all for helping me shape myself into the person I want to be. Naked, shameless, human, and free (that rhymes).

# INTRODUCTION

Do you think we are behaving as natural human beings? I believe we've become human doings. We are enslaved to money. We're not living to live; we're living to work. At least, that's what I've experienced in North America. I think we are walking a living death, reacting to our environment and circumstances. We've been doing that for thousands of years, and it's become our accepted way of being. It's one bad habit that we should collectively strive to change. I think we forget to experience what we want to experience. We take our intrinsic connection to Nature, our lives, and our bodies for granted. We never learn to realize that we have a lot to give to make this world a better place for ourselves and the people in our sphere of influence. But when we come to this realization, our lives change. Overcoming adversity is what life is about. Without adversity, life would be meaningless. Failing gets us to grow. One of the things I've learned is that I only have this moment, right now, to make a difference.

> Yesterday is history, tomorrow is a mystery, but today is a gift, and that's why it is called the present.
> —Master Oogway

Naturism is a philosophy. It has no dogma. There are some basic rules we follow, but they aren't constricting. The rules come from common sense. Simple rules like, "go ahead and look, but don't stare", "sit on a towel", and "be respectful". Not that hard, right? There are other common-sense values and behaviours which Naturists follow that I'll discuss further in the following chapters.

My gratitude towards you for reading this volume cannot be overstated. Your time is valuable, and I am so grateful that you picked up this book and decided to read it. I hope it helps to increase your awareness of who you are and how you fit into your world; that you can control your thoughts and, therefore, your life.

I am not a scholar. I'm not a learned person. I'm a Nudist who uses the term Naturist to describe my attitude towards freedom. I believe that I am part of Nature, that I am Nature personified, just like every human being in existence. I have over half a century of life experience to express on these pages, and I hope my writings will help free minds and, therefore, the world.

I'm an educator (without papers). Which means I am engaged in leading people out of ignorance. Ignorance is not knowing. I don't know how to fly a plane or bake a cake; therefore, I'm ignorant of those topics. I intend on staying that way too. I love flying, but I'm better off letting someone who loves operating a plane do it for me.

I'm an expert at fixing mechanical things. I have over forty years of experience in repairing and designing equipment. I can create procedures to follow to repair *anything* that is mechanically broken.

I'm an expert at living life. I should be. I've lived for better than six decades and have survived. I'm not perfect at it, but I get a little better at it every day by studying myself. I can help—and have helped—people live happier, healthier lives by providing them with all the information they need to change their lives, if that's what they want. What makes me an expert? Living as long as I have and employing the knowledge I've gained to change my life.

You don't necessarily have to have a university degree or a piece of wallpaper saying you've studied a particular subject at school to be an expert. An expert is someone who has studied a topic sufficiently to be able to talk about that subject with authority. I don't know if skilled fishermen with TV shows have diplomas, but they have excellent tips and tricks for landing "the big one". Would you listen to such a person if you wanted to catch fish, even though he hasn't a diploma or degree in angling?

I know, through experience, that meandering the world without purpose leads to illness. Mental illness leads to physical illness, which manifests as emotional and physical pain. I can talk with great authority on this subject. I used to consider myself the captain of the Canadian Olympic Couch Potato Team. I was a meandering meat bag—a selfish meat bag! I did whatever came next, and I was so selfish that the only things I did were the things necessary to bail me out of whatever predicament I found myself in, the plight I'd created for myself.

I used to blame my environment and circumstances for the state of my life. I'd blame anyone or anything but myself. I never took responsibility for myself. I didn't know how to do that. No one taught me until I was 51 years old. I just did what everyone else was doing. When I learned to take responsibility for myself, my life changed.

I have very learned friends. I consider them intellectuals because they have been schooled in conventional ways and clearly understand the difference between science and pseudoscience. I've known one of these people since my young-adult life, and I find what he is studying fascinating and well worth understanding. Quantum physics is a realm where I only have basic knowledge; he teaches me more at every gathering. His wife, also a very learned person, is a psychiatrist. She has abundant knowledge in her field of study and is very successful. I admire these people who can, through science and mathematics, prove theories of the existence of the Unified Field; who, through an understanding of physiology and the workings of the mind, can help struggling people.

It is my privilege to be associated with my friends. They accept me as I am. They do not try to persuade me to change my behaviour. They listen to me, and I listen to them. We have great fun discussing the secrets of the Unified Field and the mind. I miss them when we are apart, and I revel in the joy of their company when we are together.

I have studied personal development for more than ten years, and my discoveries about myself have been revealing. I have read many books on the subject and follow great new thought leaders like Tony Robins, Mel Robins, Dr. Joe Dispenza, and the man who started me on my personal development journey, Bob Proctor. These people talk about the same ideas but from their own perspectives.

I use their ideas to change my thoughts and can now state without fear that I am free.

Many more people have affected my thought processes, and I should mention them. Napoleon Hill's book, *Think and Grow Rich*, was Bob Proctor's guide from age 26 until his death in February 2022. Bob read *Think and Grow Rich* every day without fail. He considered the book his bible. Bob was a multi-millionaire at the time of his death, and his legacy will continue to be timeless and to help many people find freedom. Bob worked for Earl Nightingale, whom Napoleon Hill mentored. Bob introduced me to many writers, such as Wallace D. Wattles, James Allen, Genevieve Behrend, Thomas Troward, Raymond Holliwell, and Florence Scovel Shinn. My learned friends introduced me to Bertrand Russel and Richard Dawkins. Many more authors have helped me reshape my brain. Their ideas have allowed me to break old synaptic connections and create new ones that have brought balance and serenity into my life.

Nudism has always been part of my life. My recollection of my birth is quite fuzzy. I was very young at the time. However, I can be pretty sure that I was born naked—naked, natural, free, healthy, and alive. My mental faculties were new, and I was ignorant of their existence. I had to rely on my parents to provide all the necessities of life. All I wanted was to be loved and feel secure. Though there were some exceptions, my parents primarily employed terrible methods to help me develop and keep me on their straight and narrow path. I'll describe those later.

I hate wearing clothes. It's not natural, and it causes dis-ease. I hyphenate that word because I believe there is no such thing as disease. What I'm experiencing when I'm ill is a body that is not at ease; a body in a state of dis-ease. Illness is an inevitable result of dis-ease. Whether on the spiritual, intellectual, or physical plane, imbalance will cause dis-ease of the body, mind, or spirit. In later chapters, I'll describe my deductions on how we became a society of dis-eased bodies.

My mother often tried to embarrass me in front of my family and friends, with much success in my youth, by regaling them with stories of me, as a toddler, shedding my clothes and running down the street or beach. Now I tell that story, and I wear it like a badge of honour. I was naked, shameless, human, and free. Her ridicule didn't deter me from being naked. I think it backfired. Her determination to keep me clothed just made it fun to be rebellious. It was titillating to be naked when I knew I wasn't following the rules.

When the opportunity arises during the day to shed my skins of oppression, my body feels a deep sense of relief. I shed those sweaty, often stinky, clothes, shower away the dirt and bacteria that have accumulated on my skin, and feel rejuvenated and relaxed. When I feel that something is good and right, I know I am doing what is natural and healthy. I know when I'm doing something wrong: I feel bad before I do it and guilty after I've done it. No one has ever needed to tell me right from wrong. It's in human DNA. Religionists do not have a monopoly on morality. You can't make money from something Nature provides.

Nonsexual, communal nudity is normal and natural. When you are naked, you can do no harm, and your mind is open to accepting others for who they are, not what they are. You're more inclined to tolerate different cultures and to desire to learn about them. You're more open to forgiving differing perspectives. You're more loving and compassionate. These ideas are the essence of human life.

I believe that most humans are enslaved. We bend to the rules of others so that we can toil our lives away. We eke out an existence while the oligarchs, religionists, and their buddies—the pandering politicians—live lavishly and achieve their wealth on the backs of us, their minions.

There needs to be balance in our cultures. We've become polluting, natural-resource-plundering vermin on this planet, and Mother Earth is paying a hefty toll for our poor thinking. My goal is to help others think better. I'm not perfect at thinking, but I am trying to be a little better at it today than I was yesterday. I can confidently say that I am thinking better today than I did ten years ago.

A religionist is a controlling person. They lust for power and control over others. They use criticism and ridicule to try and shame people into behaving the way they believe their scriptures tell them all people should behave. They are self-proclaimed adjutants of God, interpreters and keepers of scripture.

A religious person believes in their scriptures without being controlled by a religionist, and accepts and tolerates other people's perspectives and beliefs.

A human being sees a person with religious beliefs and loves that person no matter their beliefs, political views, or how out of the ordinary they may behave.

I don't believe that humans are free—not as free as they think they are. I've examined my life up to this point, and I've seen things in me that I don't like. I found that I was enslaved. I was enslaved to money, and because of that, I toiled and worked hard to earn enough to meet my needs, but I never had enough to be free. Money, in my opinion, is the root cause of slavery. Avarice, the insatiable desire for material wealth or financial gain, is a human construct that has enslaved all humans. Avarice is practiced by oligarchs who pay politicians to bend to their will.

Bob Proctor and Dr Joe Dispenza made me aware that we are all energetic, or spiritual, beings on our journey back to the Unified Field. Most humans are sleepwalking, and I was no different years ago. I've had an awakening, and I want to help others wake up. I want to help people become aware of who they are and what purpose they can give themselves. Everyone is on their own path, and awareness of the journey makes a difference in a person's life.

Something that needs to be said upfront is that nudity is not the end result or the goal of being a Naturist. Nudity is a tool we use, and anyone can employ it. It helps us become comfortable with our bodies and our natural way of being. We understand there is no such thing as a perfect body; rather there is a vast variety of them. We stop judging each other because of our physical make-up. We tend to see the individual, and become more tolerant, accepting, forgiving, and loving. We stop objectifying each other. When you're naked, you're being authentic; you're not hiding behind your clothes. But you can be a Naturist with your clothes on.

My mentor taught me that there are eight billion plus brains on the planet, and no two think the exact same thoughts. Open-mindedness is essential to being a Naturist and successful in life. Being respectful to others wins your respect. It's a win-win situation when you visit a Naturist park.

The whole premise of this book is to promote reconnection physically to Mother Earth through nudity, intellectually reconnect to one's self, and spiritually reconnect to Nature. It is about being authentic to one's self, having a good body self-image, and relieving stress. Live harmoniously with everyone. Be *free*!

You'll find that I repeat myself in this book. The things I repeat are well worth reading again, so I make no apologies for it.

Please enjoy reading the book. I wish you well on your journey back to Nature.

# CHAPTER 1

# What is Nature

⸺◦⟋◦⸺

When I was but 20 years old, I looked at the world's state and wondered how humans had become so separated from the environment. I knew Nature to be the wild part of the world—the forests, lakes, rivers, streams, and oceans are places where wild animals reside. I used the term "commune with Nature" when camping or visiting a beach. Somehow I knew that humans were part of this wilderness and that we are nothing more than just another species on this planet. I knew we had an intrinsic connection to Nature even though I was taught creationism by the church I was born into. Somehow, I knew then that Nature owns us, and we cannot own anything.

But my ignorance of who I was and my place in the world didn't allow me to answer my questions of "Who am I?" and "What is my purpose?" back then. The continuous inoculation of ideas from the religious organization I had the misfortune to be born into also had a bearing on the lack of awareness I experienced for the first half of my life—brainwashed from birth. I was thinking and acting in ways other people thought and acted in order to feel accepted and loved—to "fit in". I was ridiculed, criticized, and even punished by the people who had authority over me if I acted in an unacceptable way. I was bullied because I was skinny, had no self-esteem or self-confidence, was afraid to get into trouble if I fought back, and was deathly afraid of physical harm. I was a target for the bigger and stronger boys I grew up with, and my thoughts were altered and misguided by those experiences and brainwashed by my environment and circumstances. I was an ineffective, non-thinking, insignificant lamb; caught in the flock of sheeple, looking for love and acceptance.

With my education, and I don't mean schooling, I've become aware of who I am and how I fit into this world. To me, Nature is all things and everyone. I capitalize "Nature" now because, to me, Nature is the spiritual entity that is the Universe. Some of the readers of this book will think that I am calling Nature "God". I believe that Nature was around before our solar system's dawn; before humans emerged on Mother Earth. I don't think that anyone can argue about that. We know that the Earth is greater than four billion years old—our science has proven that beyond a shadow of a doubt. We know that religious people believe that humans have existed only for a mere two thousand years. But science has proven otherwise. Yet people are conditioned to think they exist purely by the grace of a deity someone invented. This dogma has become the basis of existence for some humans.

Sitting naked beneath the trees at my favourite Naturist park, Bare Oaks, free of worry and shame, I contemplate who I am and how I fit into the bigger picture. I see the trees and flowers. I feel the air move across my naked body and hear it move through the leaves above. I hear the birds sing and see the insects crawling and flitting about on their wings. I see dogs playing or patiently being by their person's side. I smell the aromas of the flowers and food cooking on barbecues. I hear people laughing and children playing, and it all seems right. It brings me calmness and joy. I feel the grass beneath me as I lay there absorbing indirect sunlight. I feel warm and comfortable. I know that I'm cradled in the arms of Mother Earth, and I am safe. There is a sense of liberation when I shed my clothes (things I call skins of oppression).

Years ago, when I looked to see Nature, it seemed absent—hiding from my awareness. I needed to travel for hours outside of the concrete jungle I lived in to experience Nature. But now, turning to my education and knowing that I am a spiritual being gifted with six higher mental faculties, and who is manifested on this physical plane as the body I have custody of at present, I realize that Nature isn't hiding at all. Nature is me. Nature is present everywhere. Nature is found in the Universe. Nature can be seen in our galaxy. Nature can be found in all the basic building blocks found in the Universe; in all of the elements and in the atoms of molecules. Nature can be found in those atoms' electrons, protons, and neutrons. Nature can be found in the subatomic particles that make up the protons, neutrons, and electrons, and they are found *everywhere*! And because my body, the manifestation of my physical vessel, is made up of those subatomic particles, I can say, "I am Nature". Nature is everyone and everything. "Izaera" is the Basque word for Nature, and I chose that word as my writing name. I believe that I am speaking for Nature.

Being naked in public is as natural as being born. Being naked and physically connected to Mother Earth is liberating and calming. Shedding my skins of oppression after a long day of living to work, my body thanks me and returns to a calm, relaxed, and stressless state. It's as if Nature were saying "I see you now, and you are real. You are secure. You have nothing to worry about."

Nature and the Universe are the same thing. The Universe, the Unified Field, the Force, or whatever deity you believe in are all the same. Nature is the energy that links and glues all things and everyone together. If humans unified their belief in Nature, we could find common ground to rally around. We could unite together if we saw the human before us instead of seeing our physical, religious, or intellectual differences. We can believe in Nature because we are Nature. We are evidence that Nature is real.

Nature is pure love. It has no malice. It creates. It grows. It expresses itself by manifesting the beauty of the Universe, which I am in awe of. The growth Nature does is seen in how all species evolve and populate Mother Earth. Nature's growth is evident in the expansion of our known Universe. Nature's growth is apparent in how many seeds Mother Earth's plants produce.

The Universe is constantly expanding and growing. New galaxies and solar systems pop up every second. Growth in balance is what Nature makes. Nature provides methods of keeping balance on Mother Earth. Every species on Mother Earth is here to balance every other species. Humans are here as part of that balance. Proof of Nature's existence can be seen in Mother Earth and in every species in existence.

What is Nature? Nature is a form of energy that exists at such a high frequency that it is impossible to register or detect it with mechanical or electronic means. It is all things and everyone. It is all places and everywhere. It has always been and will always be. It cannot be created or destroyed. It can only be transmuted from one form of energy to the next.

Everything in this physical realm we call reality is gravitationally organized light and information. All things and all species are the same. Energy reduces in vibration to form animate and inanimate objects. The human form is this energy reduced in frequency to a level where it coalesces into physical form.

Humans have dishonoured Nature by clothing our bodies and making them sick. We have evolved slowly, and only now, in recent times, have we learned to control our thinking and our behaviour. There is still way more to learn and many people to educate. But the global consciousness is awakening, and things are shifting in the right direction. People are learning how to think and are giving up on archaic ways of thinking. We are starting to understand that we can control our thoughts.

It took us millions of years to get here. Now we need to learn from our past and apply what we've learned to progress further and faster. It's time for us to return to our roots and become human beings again, helping each other instead of competing against each other.

# CHAPTER 2

# The Big Separation

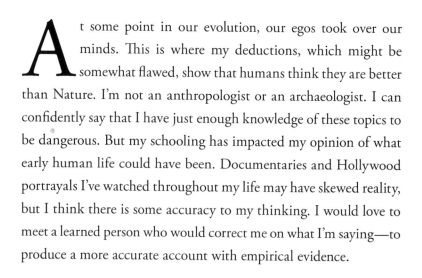

At some point in our evolution, our egos took over our minds. This is where my deductions, which might be somewhat flawed, show that humans think they are better than Nature. I'm not an anthropologist or an archaeologist. I can confidently say that I have just enough knowledge of these topics to be dangerous. But my schooling has impacted my opinion of what early human life could have been. Documentaries and Hollywood portrayals I've watched throughout my life may have skewed reality, but I think there is some accuracy to my thinking. I would love to meet a learned person who would correct me on what I'm saying—to produce a more accurate account with empirical evidence.

I know that the ego is a mental entity that aids our survival. Our experiences and environment, tens of thousands of years ago, caused our egos to believe that fighting for what we want is the only way to survive. As an example, at some point we started to think "my food", "my land", "my water", and "my mate". Ownership is what we created. We discovered that we could use violence to protect all we thought was ours. We used violence to ensure others knew when we disagreed with their behaviour. This probably started before we had language to communicate our displeasure of unacceptable behaviour.

I think that in today's world, using violence to change the behaviour of the masses is immoral. Using violence has always been met with resistance, escalating violence into acts of retribution. We can communicate effectively now. But we haven't learned tolerance, acceptance, and forgiveness, and we certainly do not love all people unconditionally yet.

The human construct of competition came to be because of these egoic survival concepts: we felt it necessary to protect what we thought was ours. Before ownership and competition, we would share what we had. We gave love, and helped each other survive, be at peace, and be happy. We'd play all day long. We played at gathering things; we played at hunting; we played at building shelters and looking after our families. We were at peace.

But ownership and competition corrupted living. Heaven forbid a neighbour from across the river should come to "my side of the river" and gather "my firewood" for his needs. (I doubt they thought "heaven forbid" because heaven hadn't been invented then.) We'd throw rocks or make loud, threatening noises to scare them away, and if need be, we'd shed blood. Barbaric? No, natural. Our egos evolved this way.

"That guy on the other side of the river and his family smell funny and are hairier with big long fangs sticking out of their mouths. They don't walk as tall as we do, so we're better than them." We started to see differences between each other. We learned to use those differences to justify defending what we thought was ours and violently enforce our beliefs of ownership. Ownership and separation started to invade our minds.

Competition sucked up a lot of our energy. We knew that hunting was necessary and that killing another species to supply us with food was required. I find it odd that we felt good when we committed acts of violence, but I think it is a construct of the ego that we should be violent if necessary. I think the joy of having meat to eat translated into the act of violence that provided the food. And when we felt threatened by someone invading *our territory* (ownership), we acted violently to prevent it, which felt good. Immoral as hell, but it still felt good.

Protecting our families and communities from people who would try to control us is OK, but we've gotten used to using violence to settle disputes. We should be ashamed of that now, and make every effort to eliminate violence. Violence is perpetuated by the films that Hollywood creates. It's perpetuated by the violent video games our children play. I cannot understand the need for violence and how people can sleep at night profiting from it.

What would the world have been like if we had co-created instead of competed? The guy from the other side of the river came over to our side, and we said, "Yup, you're ugly, you stink, you have fangs, and it's OK! We see you're foraging and need food, so come over and let's sit down and find out about each other and share our bounty." What if we overlooked our differences and helped each other because we wanted to and because it feels way better than being violent? My question is, can we change our ways, or is it too late?

We were also curious critters. Why does it rain? Why does it get cold? Why are there fluffy white things (clouds) floating above me? Why do the leaves change colours and fall to the ground? Where does lightning come from? Great questions. The elders of the communities started to use their ability to deduce answers. Science was in its infancy, and deduction was the primary tool.

The wise elder deduced the answers by creating supernatural entities—inventions of our ignorant but growing minds. The gods of thunder and lightning. The gods of cyclical events. "The god of the inexplicable yet observable phenomena that must have a cause or reason to happen by that god's whim and for *his* pleasure, and because of *his* disappointment, punishment is doled out." I like the name of that god! It sounds like a Monty Python sketch. These wise elders became very powerful, and started dictating community behaviour and what rituals to practice through constant, consistent, spaced repetition reinforced by ridicule, criticism, coercion, and, if deemed necessary, corporal punishment or, worse, violence. These ideas became dogma that has lasted for thousands of years. They used deities as a "higher authority" to which all humans would answer. The masses feared this higher authority, and the self-appointed representatives of these deities wielded power over the people.

The sudden death of someone would be attributed to a deity. "Oh, they did something bad, and now the gods are balancing things out." Maybe someone was attacked and eaten by a sabre-toothed whatchamacallit. "Oh, that person," says the elder, "misbehaved, and the gods got angry and sent the sabre-toothed whatchamacallit to punish them."

Thus controlism made its appearance in our psychology. The shaman, medicine man, and priest became very powerful indeed. They were the master interpreters of the acts of Nature (er … I mean the gods) and, therefore, became authority figures. They bent the ears of the tribal elders, the leaders; and then, millennia later, kings and queens, emperors, feudal lords, tsars, kaisers, royalty; and, even later, dictators, presidents, and prime ministers. These politicians would become accustomed to pandering to religious leaders to quiet the noise they made and, by pandering to them, buy their way into heaven.

Here I must add that I use the term "religionist" to describe an immoral person who would forcibly project their wishes and desired behaviour onto other humans. I say immoral because those religionists are infringing on the rights of others when they use coercion, ridicule, criticism, and violence to force people to behave as they dictate. To me, a religious person studies and understands religious scriptures without proselytizing or infringing on the rights of others. These are good, well-meaning people that the religionists may misguide. However, when a religious person becomes militant and tries to force their beliefs on others, the religionists control that person. Such a person is a danger to the remainder of the population.

Shame is another construct that religionists use to control human behaviour. It has caused greater separation from Nature.

They devised rules to live by, and introduced shame for not abiding by the rules. "Nudity is the work of the devil." "Questioning our authority is blasphemy." "Opposing the institution and protesting is heresy." "You should be ashamed of your behaviour and yourself!" Shame is a form of criticism. This is only one trick they use to cause us to conform to their narrow-minded, archaic ideology and practices. They have never changed those practices to keep pace with our evolving consciousness. Napoleon Hill's book *Outwitting the Devil* details these hustlers and snake-oil salesmen who do no good for humanity.

The emotion that is felt is guilt, not shame. There is no such emotion as shame in a human. We were not born with shame. We were inoculated with it by the religionists through our parents, schools, and laws. They would shame us for being naked and natural. They would shame us for dancing naked by firelight during the various solstices. They would shame us for playing naked beach volleyball. They would shame us for breathing if the mood struck them. They killed people because those people worshipped Nature and looked after Mother Earth. That is immorality in its highest form. Shame is shameful. We were not born to conform but to *stand out and shine!*

Someone wrote the line at some point, and I paraphrase it here: and *man* shall have dominion over all things created. Those words widened the big separation between humans, Nature, and Mother Earth. You can tell that it was the male ego that wrote it. I think it's a foul concept. A woman would never have thought of it. Females are way more compassionate and empathetic, and their egos are nowhere as small as that of males. They are more likely to want to co-create instead of competing. Women should occupy the highest offices of government, business, and schools; then we would have peace in the world.

I believe the original line has been bastardized by a few egotistical men who then forced the idea into the minds of others, causing them to behave in a way that goes against Nature and allows people to plunder the natural resources of Mother Earth. I believe the original line was "People have dominion over all things created in their minds." When you think about it clearly, humans have no dominion over anything. Nature has dominion over all things and everyone. Nature will take back everything humans can create, including humans themselves.

Humans have dominion over one thing and one thing alone—their thoughts and their process of thinking. The problem here, though, is that 95 per cent of the world's population does not think. They are not consciously aware of what they are thinking. The controlists know this and take advantage of humans by proselytizing, and those humans that would believe the controlists would then have the authority to disavow Nature and plunder Mother Earth.

Dogma is a militant evil that sees competition in anything or anyone that disagrees. It would use violence to silence opposition. It considers diversity as a threat to its security. Dogma would force us to believe things without questioning what the dogmatists, religionists, politicians, and oligarchs tell us to believe. Dogma creates most of the unrest in the world. Dogma has created the ability to see differences in others and provided the criteria for judgement.

Followers of dogma have relinquished their ability to think for themselves, given their very existence to the religionists, oligarchs, and politicians. They believe that life is a dress rehearsal for the afterlife—an idea that the religionists created. Life is the only time we can be conscious. We must live diligently to enjoy our journey and to make our lives valuable to others.

The religionists use fear as a weapon to control behaviour. People who believe them walk their lives in fear. The fear of death is their primary trick of control. They'll have people think that there is an afterlife, and in that afterlife, there are only two destinations—one positive and one negative. They'll tell people to behave in specific ways to gain entry to the positive side. Still, more often than not, they'll describe the negative side in great detail in order to place fear in people's minds; to explain that behaving in any other manner than what they say will result in eternal damnation to that negative place.

I have witnessed people on the last days of their lives praying that they'll go to the positive side, being in such fear of the negative side. What a foulness the religionists create in the minds of people. People should never fear death. They should celebrate every moment they are conscious, and live joyfully. But that's not what the religionists want. They can't control people without fear. They can't fill their coffers if people live in harmony and joy rather than fear. By the way, if anyone tells you that they know what happens after we die, they are either a liar or a fool. Dogmatists, religionists, oligarchs, and pandering politicians are those fools and liars.

The religionists know that the best time to implant their dogma in the mind of a person is when that person has just arrived on Mother Earth. The mind of a newborn child is like a sponge. It listens to and views events surrounding it, and feels the emotions and vibrations of those near it. It absorbs all that is in its awareness. What better time is there to corrupt a mind? Religionists don't like people who are aware and who think. These people diminish their power, so they work diligently to program young minds through the constant repetition of their dogma. How immoral is this? The separation from Nature widens with each corrupted mind.

After a certain age, the oligarchs take over. They, too, know that programming a young mind is the best time to create the minions they need to do the work in their factories and offices. They start with children who enter kindergarten. The schools are their tool for creating these minions. Don't get me wrong, I think the people, the teachers, are magnificent, loving, and genuinely well-meaning people stuck in a corrupt system. Schools were set up by fascists in the late 1800s to produce mindless, obedient, enslaved people for their factories and businesses. Once again, children are taught what to think, not how to think. Free thinkers are a detriment to the wallets of the greedy rich oligarchs, the religionists, and the politicians. So teaching children how to think is catastrophic for controlling the masses. The schools are built on archaic concepts that have stayed the same over the past 100-plus years. Children are punished for not following the rules. The separation continues to be perpetuated for another generation. People become human doings and are not allowed to know how to be human beings.

And then there's money. A valuable metal is given in exchange for services or goods. Before money, bartering was an appropriate method of exchange. "I'll provide my service for so many chickens." Trading. We still trade today. We trade time for money. Money was another method for the greedy rich to control the behaviour of the masses. The banks were born, and the inventors found a way to get something for nothing. Exchanging your gold coins for paper money, you were given 67 per cent of the value of your gold for paper with a denomination printed on it. Paper money has never been worth anything more than paper.

The greedy rich also control us (I'll discuss this in greater detail later). Humans have always searched for ways to accumulate wealth without giving a fair equivalent in return. Criminals work on the same premise. How can I get something for nothing? This goes against Nature's law. There is no such thing as something for nothing.

Givers understand that if they give their talents freely, without expecting any compensation, they receive abundantly. They also know that the more they give, the more they'll receive. Bob Proctor taught me to give freely and receive graciously; this idea has significantly impacted my life. If everyone learned to think this way, mending Mother Earth would be an undertaking made by all, and global peace could be had.

The only way to become human beings again, as opposed to human doings, is to reconnect to Nature and become custodians of Mother Earth. Living life naked, being true to ourselves, shedding the skins of oppression, and relinquishing the false pretences we try to use to impress each other brings true freedom.

I cannot express how important it is to teach children *how* to think and eliminate teaching them *what* to think. Free thinking will liberate the world. Free thinking will end poverty, starvation, competition, and slavery.

Nudity is real freedom. Being truthful and authentic, naked as the day we were born, is liberating. Happiness is guaranteed when you are naked in a community of naked people—connecting and socializing in real time, not virtually. Health and happiness are increased by living a naked life. Co-creating naked businesses, naked events, naked social media, and naked living with others is the ultimate way to reconnect to Nature and bring balance back to Mother Earth.

Not all Nudists or Naturists are consciously aware of what they are thinking, but they know that to get along in a community, they must express tolerance, acceptance, forgiveness, and above all, love.

Nudism and Naturism are a path to peace and prosperity, and if you have never experienced naked living, you are missing out on one of the most liberating and peaceful states of being there is. There's a simple and safe way to start. If you're at home, take your clothes off. If you live alone, that's easy. If you have family members around you, start a conversation about nudity in the house being tolerable, and start shedding your skins of oppression. Watch how fast your family members join in. Have frank discussions about nudity, and desexualize the act of being naked and the human body. Your life will never be the same.

We have only this very moment in time to experience all that we want to experience. We have only this moment in time to take action and create the results and circumstances we want. To give our lives to the religionists and oligarchs by thinking and living as they dictate or force us to live is a sin of epic proportions. To waste our lives trying to live up to the expectations of religionists, oligarchs, and politicians is detrimental to our success as a species and to our personal health. Take responsibility for yourself. Start to think. Liberate yourself from the conformity and mundanity of living according to the masses. Close the big separation and reconnect to Nature. Take care of Mother Earth, and we will all benefit.

Live happy and free. You have nothing to lose except your clothes.

# CHAPTER 3

# The New Mind

I experienced a situation which made me wonder how parents influence the mind of a newborn child. When a person arrives, they have the gift of intellect well within reach, but none of the six higher mental faculties have had a chance to develop. The faculty of reason is so new that whatever the infant is exposed to is absorbed like a dry sponge immersed in water for the first time. Everything it hears, sees, tastes, touches, and smells has an uncontrolled and direct path to its subconscious mind. When it develops, the reasoning faculty allows the child to determine what is true and real and what is false and wrong. But the time before the reasoning faculty has grown is when they are most vulnerable to positive or negative ideas. Tactile and emotional, or vibrational, stimuli influence infants more than words. If a parent is angry or frustrated, the child receives the vibration of those emotions, which causes the child to feel unsafe. The child's poor behaviour may increase. But if the parent is in love and can show compassion and empathy, the child feels those vibrations and, therefore, feels safe and secure.

I was born and grew up during the 1960s. I was born into a family that wasn't great at communicating. My parents immigrated from Germany and Austria shortly after World War II. They grew up with a maniacal, insane man as head of the country; who used propaganda, lies, coercion, and violence to control the population. They were also born into religious families, and had a lot of fear and insecurity because of the rules they had to try to live up to. They inoculated me with the same ideas and rules before I had developed my higher faculty of reason and could determine what was real, true, wrong, and false for myself. This was an era where Comstock and Spock were significant influences on the people of North America. Others of the extreme right-wing political and moral minority did an immense amount of damage to our culture. We were surreptitiously enslaved to ideas that violated our human rights even more than living under the rule of a tyrant.

Growing up with my mom and dad, I learned how to be a parent. I knew they did their best with what they were programmed, but I also knew that I did not want to bring a child into this world so that I could treat it the same way my parents treated me. I love my parents. I don't blame them for the illness I suffered for 51 years. I've learned a lot about myself in the past ten years, and I've matured and have become responsible for myself and my behaviour. I'm on a path to freedom. I still react to my environment and circumstances, but the reactions are short-lived, and I'm starting to respond to what's happening now better and better.

I observed a young mother sitting on a park bench with her daughter, whom I placed at about two years old. The baby was crying and fussy, and the mother was holding her daughter on her lap and trying so hard not to lose her composure. Mom had this very stoic, stone-faced look. She was bottling up her emotions, which was detrimental to her well-being. I imagined what was going through her mind was "Please, child, stop this nonsense". I felt sorry for the mom but more so for the child.

I have no idea what the child was being so fussy about. Her mind had not developed enough to communicate her thoughts, which frustrated the parent. But the child, being caught up in herself and unable to understand what was going on, could still feel the tension from her mother. I think this interaction could exacerbate the child's feelings and, therefore, her behaviour would worsen.

I'm not a parent, and I am glad I made that choice, not because of selfishness but because I knew long ago that I would have been a lousy parent. My anger and frustration would have been something I expressed too quickly and would have been so detrimental to my children's mental and emotional growth. But with my awakening and self-study, I think I would now be an *awesome* parent.

I wondered what the child's reaction would have been to her mom asking questions like "Hey! What's going on? What are you feeling right now?" The little girl wouldn't have been able to articulate her feelings in words. Still, I think that redirecting her thoughts from being caught in her emotional state to becoming aware of her emotional state would have gotten her to stop being fussy and pay attention to what she was feeling. I think that if Mom had felt compassion for her daughter and tried to console her by saying "It's OK, you're not in trouble, you're safe here in my arms, and whatever you are feeling is OK. I just want you to be aware of what you are feeling." This would have done more to calm her daughter than any candy, toy, or smartphone could ever do. It would have also kickstarted her child into being aware of her feelings and soon, once her mind developed more, mindful of her thoughts.

I wonder if there have been any studies of such redirection of very young minds. It would be interesting to see what results were found.

A new mind has only love to express. It hasn't learned how to be malicious or provoke or manipulate. It only gives love of the purest nature. All it wants in return is to be loved, safe, and free. As it matures, its experiences and lessons from authorities in their environment taint their thoughts and, if done incorrectly, create doubt and worry, two mental dis-eases that hinder the mind's growth. Worry and doubt, if not expressed, can turn into anger which, if turned inward, becomes depression.

Exposing a young mind to corruptive influences is dangerous at this point in early life. People often do not take responsibility for the new minds they bring into the world. Parents owe everything they have to that new mind. They must protect it from influences that would stunt its mental and spiritual growth. It is pure selfishness if a parent places a smartphone in the hands of a child under the age of reason to entertain that child. If the parent were selfless and used their time to be with that child, educating it, that child would grow to be an incredible force in the world.

Remember we reside on three planes of existence simultaneously. We are spiritual beings, gifted with intellect, and manifested in this 3D realm we call reality in the physical form of our bodies. There is balance when a person is aware of all three planes and devotes equal attention to them. The body can be at ease. The mind can also be at ease because there is balance in the intellect. The spirit is free to express itself, and with that comes fulfilment.

Because an underdeveloped mind is like a sponge, religionists can take free thinking away from a human. If too much attention is placed on one plane of existence, an imbalance in that life happens. Where there is an imbalance, there is dis-ease. The power-lusting people, religionists, oligarchs, and pandering politicians all know there is the power to control people where there is dis-ease. Religionists, more than anyone else, know that placing fear into the minds of the masses is a way to control them. They know that taking control of a mind must occur shortly after they are born.

Humans spend too much time being emotional, and must be more mindful of their emotional state. Most humans, including religionists, oligarchs, and pandering politicians, are consumed by their physical being and world. They don't think about the spiritual being or using their intellectual faculties correctly at all. We often get caught in negative emotional states because we react to our circumstances and environment and get caught in a negative, reactive doom cycle. I can attest to this because this was precisely my condition over ten years ago. I was losing my cool at the drop of a hat, embracing negative emotions and attracting more to worry about into my life. I was sick.

We tend to close our hearts when we get stung by life's unpleasantries. When we stop feeling, we stop connecting to Mother Earth, Nature, and each other. What a shame that is. When I say closing our hearts, I don't mean arresting the feeling of love; I mean avoiding all emotions. But avoiding taking the risk of loving is the worst thing we can do. The secret to feeling loved by others is to love everyone and everything, no matter how anyone or anything treats you. I hear you say "*impossible!*" It is not impossible. It takes practice and emotional awareness to recognize that a button has been pushed and to know how to respond and not react.

If a young mind is taught to be aware of its emotions, that thoughts create feelings, that mind becomes strong and resistant to negative influences. Its reasoning faculty proliferates, and it is more able to discern between true and real things, and false and wrong things.

How do we teach a young mind to be free? Lavish them with love. Spread it on thick, like peanut butter on toast. Love that mind with all your heart and show it is safe no matter what it's feeling. Teach it to be aware of its feelings, and to respond to external stimuli, and control its reactions. It will react, and sometimes it will react incorrectly. But it will also learn from its mistakes and be more capable of responding when circumstances it doesn't initially like arise. It's always better to recognize when things don't feel right and that the first reaction may cause more issues. Teach them to stand back and say "that's interesting"; to think about the emotional state being experienced and ask "What's going on? How do I feel in this reactive state? How do I change my emotional state to understand this experience?"

What a powerful mind that would be indeed.

Imagine if our schools would teach how to think instead of what to think. One generation of minds taught how to think, and the world would be at peace.

Nudists and Naturists, being open-minded, are great people to create environments to nurture the young and start them co-creating the peaceful world we all crave. We're not better at raising children, but I do believe that Naturist children grow up with more open minds. They are less corrupted by clothed ideals and have fewer sexual hang-ups as well.

Some studies align with those statements. Margaret Mead studied an Indigenous tribe of people in the South Pacific and how they lived without guilt and anxiety, could choose when to cover up and what to wear, and were free. Wouldn't it be nice to shed guilt and anxiety as quickly as shedding our skins of oppression?

Having suffered from anxiety and panic attacks for most of my life, I know that being naked isn't the only cure for anxiety. But being authentic, not trying to fit into a box of normal that isn't mine, helped me relieve my stress. My anxiety is no more than a pang that I can recognize, and with some practice, I've learned that I can switch it off.

# CHAPTER 4

# The Environment

———⌇———

Humans have six higher mental faculties that separate us from all other species. If you look at the other species, they are perfect. They blend into their environment. They take what they need, and they give what they can. They live in balance. They don't worry about anything. They only get stressed if they become prey and when they are chased. Short periods of stress are followed by long periods of ease.

Humans, with our higher mental faculties, can change our environment. If we need shelter, we build it. If we need warmth, we create a controlled fire. We want to sit on something comfortable, so we make a chair. All of these things we get from the resources that Mother Earth provides. We don't ask to use them; we take them. And because there are no protests from the other species or Mother Earth, we keep taking them. We got used to using the natural resources that Mother Earth provides. We got so used to it that we started to over-consume these resources.

There is the wild, villages, towns, and cities. All are environments owned by Nature, but humans created most, and Mother Earth pays the price. Mother Earth is ill, and humans are the virus that made her sick. Thinking is the inoculation that will eliminate the virus, and humans will become symbiotic elements of the natural workings of Mother Earth.

Native North Americans have a saying: "Use what you need and leave the rest." Indigenous people are guardians of Mother Earth. We can learn a lot from their way of life. For some egotistical reasons, we ignore these people or treat them poorly. Our Western culture is not a good one, to be sure. I admit to having a limited engagement with Native North Americans, and know little about their culture, but it makes me wonder if they would be naked if Western civilization had not interfered with their way of life.

I believe it's an environmental issue. I live in a cooler climate and have engaged with Indigenous people here in a minimal way. They have magnificent costumes they wear when they celebrate their culture. Otherwise, they dress much the same as the rest of us, something that was beaten into their culture when arrogant Westerners arrived on these shores. I'm sure that in warmer climates, they tend to wear less. But for some reason, they prefer not to live naked. I want to meet a Native North American person who could educate me on their culture.

Humans are an incredible species on Mother Earth. We are, however, just another species. As such, we have a natural desire to conserve energy. We don't want to expend more calories than what we take in. That's not conducive to good health. So, though we must work off those calories to be healthy, we tend to consider methods of getting something for nothing to conserve calories. Unfortunately, that goes against universal laws. There is no such thing as something for nothing. This is like sitting beside the fire pit, expecting warmth, without finding the wood to put into it. "Give me the heat, and I'll supply the wood." That will leave one waiting to be warm for an extended period.

We find it easier to let others supply us with food than to go foraging and share what we've acquired. We've created businesses around this concept. We pay for the food with money. And we pay taxes on that food, which is our government getting something for nothing. We build great big concrete jungles that we infest like viruses. We plunder Mother Earth's resources to shelter us and keep us warm. We over-consume everything. We want instant gratification, a mental illness constructed by our avarice. Financial institutions take advantage of this mental dis-ease and offer us free money in the form of credit cards, which is another way for banks and financial institutions to enslave humans.

You see credit-card salespeople in grocery and department stores. You hear credit advertisements on the radio and streaming audio apps. You see advertisements on TV, social media, and YouTube. "Here's some free money so you can buy what you want immediately!" But what they don't tell you is the astronomical interest rate you get charged for the privilege of using their money. The rates are so big, and the financial institutions are gambling on you creating such deep credit debt that you cannot pay off the loan quickly, and the interest they earn is something for nothing. That is immorality at its finest. Avarice is their poison to humanity. They are tricksters and enslavers.

Nudists and Naturists build a community based on helping each other. As a small example, I'm a novice volleyball player. I have a desire to get better at controlling the ball. Four fellow Naturists and I were trying to practice on a beach court at Bare Oaks, and out of the blue, another Naturist came along and offered to coach us. This young woman is a fantastic player. I've watched her play in tournaments, and she astounds me with her abilities. For her to offer to help is a real blessing. She didn't do it for money. She didn't do it for prestige. She did it because she felt good about doing it. This is the essence of co-creation. A natural way for humans to express themselves and find fulfilment. I asked her how we could compensate her for her efforts, and she only said, "Just get better at playing." I am overwhelmed with gratitude for the friendship of this beautiful spirit.

Farming has become an industrial entity. Instead of farming to provide for local communities, we farm for profits. There needs to be thought given to replenishing the soils our food grows in. Currently, farming is about getting as much growth from the soil as possible without spending money on providing proper nutrients to the soil our food comes from. Yields are enormous, but the food isn't as nutritious as it once was because the dirt it's grown in has no nutritional elements. Decades of industrial farming have ruined Mother Earth. Dirt, once living soil, is washed away by rains and ends up in the rivers, streams, lakes, and eventually oceans. Living soil contains microbial life forms, which provide nutrients to the soil that plants and humans need to be healthy and grow. It is not economical to replenish the dirt with high-quality natural nutrients or create a living biome that absorbs and retains water. Industrial farmers would rather make money instead of nutritious food.

Industrial farming, in my opinion, is environmental murder. Genetically modified organisms are immoral. Humans have no right to de-evolve the genetic perfection of any other species to create profit. Greedy chemical companies make it impossible for farmers to do an ethical job of providing food for consumption by any species. The herbicides and pesticides used in industrial farming are murdering the microbial species that live in the soil and put nutrients back into the soil again. The ignorance of farmers who don't study Nature's ways of producing crops without poisons is surprising. Industrial farmers are just the vehicles of this murderous approach. Avarice of the giant chemical companies is at the bottom of this. Pandering politicians empower these companies, and the humans will soon pay by starving to death. Nature always works in balance, and humans are disrupting that balance. Nature will bring balance back to Mother Earth, even if it means starving us to death.

A huge company that would endeavour to change Nature's perfection is guilty of immorality against Mother Earth and should be held accountable. Their lust for money and opulence is immoral. How much is enough? How are these companies helping Mother Earth sustain humans? They're not. They're sustaining their wallets—humans be damned!

If farmers returned to natural farming, the benefits would be tenfold: more nutritious food for their customers; higher yields with healthier soil. All species of Mother Earth would benefit. The environment would be cleaner. There would be fewer chemicals in our food, streams, rivers, lakes, and oceans; cleaner air with fewer greenhouse gases. Just a great, clean, healthy environment for future generations. The huge chemical companies that currently enslave farmers would not be able to survive, and that, too, is good for Mother Earth.

I appeal to farmers to let go of their dependency on chemical companies and stand on their own feet to benefit all species. Ask yourself, how much is enough?

Humans have created environments that allow us to be safe, sheltered, and comfortable and expend no more energy than required to survive. But we have also created illnesses that we shouldn't be experiencing. By forcing humans to wear clothes—for the benefit of no one but the controlists—and by building shelters that block out the sun, controlists have depleted the human body of a natural nutrient called vitamin D. Vitamin D is incredibly important to our bodies; without enough of it, the body's ability to prevent many illnesses—such as heart, lung, and kidney disease, cancer, and osteoporosis—is impaired. There is more likelihood of contracting mental illness as well.

The natural way for humans to traverse our physical realm is to be naked in it. Natural vitamin D is created by and regulated by the skin when exposed to sunlight. By clothing our bodies for whatever controlist thoughts we were inoculated with, we decrease our body's ability to be healthy. Supplementation, placing chemicals into our bodies, is the only way to increase vitamin D levels. There is the possibility of overdosing using these chemicals and again creating dis-ease of the body.

The stress encountered by the belief that nudity is immoral or dirty is outrageous and sexualizes the human body. These thought programs given to us at a young age keep us ill and in slavery to the oligarchs and religionists.

To live in the concrete jungles, we are forced to be who we are not. We wear clothes—not clothes we want to wear, but clothes that we think are acceptable to the people in our communities—to feel as if we fit in with the rest of the sheeple. Religionists and oligarchs are again at the root of these abominable ideas, and laws created to enforce them create illness and separation. They benefit no one except those who lust for power and profits.

Imagine if everyone were naked. The human form would be normalized. Sexual tension wouldn't be created by imaginary sexual ideas but by actual participation in sexual acts, which every individual could control if we taught people how to think. Religionists and oligarchs would lose their power to control us. Violence would likely be less. People would be at ease, healthy, genuine, and authentic. They would likely be thinking about ways to work together instead of competing.

The concrete jungles humans have built over the decades are also based on avarice. Who benefits from the development of these jungles? Not Nature, not humans, but oligarchs.

Oligarchs know that there is the ability to control people where there is illness and separation. They support the terrible ideas of modesty and shame to maintain control over the masses. They invest in developing these concrete jungles to control the masses, and use them to benefit their businesses and opulent lifestyles.

We have created stressful environments. False urgency, just-in-time delivery of products, and time-sensitive work are just a few things in our environments that cause stress in the human body. The human construct of trading time for money is another illness causing dis-ease in the human body. In North America, we live to work. We think that success means working harder and harder and not enjoying life. We believe that if we work hard for forty or fifty years, we can retire to do what we want. Unfortunately that leads to what is known as saturation. We can only work so hard before we run into diminishing returns. We work hard for all those years, and in the end, we have very little to show for our efforts. We can only do so much before we start using more energy than we have to give. We can only do so much during the day, and we soon get sick from putting out too much energy. We soon pay for trying to earn. Whether it's with our health or financial difficulties, we pay. It has never been a good way of living or a good way of thinking. Businesses fail because of this flawed thinking. Humans die because of these foul concepts. How much is enough? Co-creation is the pressure release of these hostile environments.

Our environments have been built on big business concepts and their greed. The controlists, the people that the politicians pander to, know that keeping people ill in their bodies and using the school systems to create minions for their factories and office buildings will bring them significant dividends. Humans pay a hefty price for survival, which is unnatural and certainly not equitable.

Criminality is also a learned concept created by the environment of inequality and non-equitability. The criminal mind sees injustice in the environment our controlists—oligarchs, religionists, and pandering politicians—have created. They feel justified in taking what they want without guilt. But they, too, infringe on the rights of others, and as I stated before, that's immoral. Criminals are humans that do not know who they are and live small meaningless lives. They react to their circumstances and seek ways to get something for nothing. They create an environment where children are taught to take without concern about infringing on others' rights. It is the extreme of small-mindedness.

Here's the concept that changed my life. I can change my environment by moving my body from one place to another. However, I bring my circumstances to the new environment, which will start to look like the old one after a brief period if I don't try to change my thinking. My actions generate a reaction from my environment, attracting more of the same circumstances. Thoughts create feelings, feelings create actions, and actions create results. I've changed my thinking. I no longer live in worry and doubt as I was programmed to do from birth. I now have a vision of the future I want to experience, and I'm becoming the person I need to be to manifest it. It is challenging work, to be sure, but it is fun and well worth the effort, and the work is never-ending. I'm on a path of lifelong learning, and I love it.

We need to create an environment that is free and open to all. We need to lose old business concepts of bottom-line obsession and start the new idea of co-creation. We need to give before we get, and giving increases returns. The more people we serve, the more rewards we receive. We must control our behaviour to take power away from the controlists. Making good decisions, like when it is appropriate to go bare, what to wear when it isn't, and controlling our sexual expression, will liberate us from the control of oligarchs, religionists, and pandering politicians.

That takes work. It takes learning how to think and practicing these methods of thought control. No one can make anyone think anything they don't want to think. Therefore we need to teach people the ways of controlling their thoughts. It's easy to understand and fun, but it will sometimes be the most challenging work anyone can undertake. Still, with persistence, a desire for achievement, and an unfailing will, the world will see peace and prosperity for all.

I hereby put the oligarchs, religionists, and pandering politicians on notice that their time is short. They must adjust their ways to survive or quietly ride off into the sunset. I prefer the latter. I'll provide transportation in the form of old camels for their departure. That's how they arrived; that's how they can leave. Goodbye. Good riddance.

Naked and free is all that humanity wants to be.

# CHAPTER 5

# Wealth vs Greed

———⌁———

I love being a Naturist. I think I have a better handle on what it means to be wealthy because of my association with naked people. There is nothing wrong with being wealthy. Wealth isn't necessarily having more money than you need and hoarding it. Wealth is having good health, being happy, and having enough money to be free by meeting one's basic needs and using what's left to benefit humanity.

Wealth is being free of spirit and feeling happy and fulfilled. It's being selfless and freely giving one's talents and abilities with love and compassion. It's expressing one's creativity, uncensored without fear. It's being free and joyful. And should the rewards for living such a life bring monetary wealth, it was earned by giving services or products to people who want them and use them.

Wealthy people give way more in "use value" than they receive in "monetary value" for their products and services.

Wealthy people are passionate about helping others be wealthy. They give their talents and abilities to those who need them freely and without expecting anything in return. Wealthy people understand and apply the principle of co-creation by creating products or services that benefit people and can help people be prosperous.

Wealthy people are filled with love and generosity.

Wealthy people have no problem showing vulnerability.

Wealthy people have a high sense of morality, never infringing on the rights of others.

Wealthy people are in control of their thinking.

Wealthy people display happiness and kindness. They show compassion and a willingness to be helpful.

Wealthy people are a joy to be in the company of.

Wealthy people stay calm and poised in the face of adversity or when facing challenges. They co-create solutions to challenges and allow others to use their talents and abilities to manifest great results.

Wealthy people nurture employees and help them grow as human beings. Wealthy people see their employees as assets and invest in them.

Wealthy people give generously and receive graciously.

There is no such thing as something for nothing. That is a universal law. Taking without giving doesn't work. Loving money more than people will not bring peace or comfort to anyone.

Religionists, oligarchs, and corrupt, pandering politicians are examples of people who would enslave humans to line their pockets and fill their bank accounts.

Avarice is a vile and abusive state of mind. It causes humans to enslave humans.

Banks enslave hard-working individuals. They ply methods like giving credit so that people accumulate insurmountable and unrepayable debt. Banks treat their employees poorly, and have a high attrition rate and employee turnaround. Banking is greed on open display. Pandering politicians create laws that make banking necessary to keep track of the poor, hard-working public and tax them for their labour. Banks are obsessed with their bottom lines, and should they fail to accrue a given amount of profit that was not as great as their previous quarter, they say they have lost money. Greed is in their words. They haven't lost money; they didn't make as much.

Religionists and oligarchs make minions out of beautiful well-meaning people who want nothing more than to be free and fearless. They use pandering politicians to create the curriculum presented by schools, and the schools make minions out of the students for the oligarch's businesses. Politicians pander to the oligarchs and continuously bleed the masses to keep them in fear and separation—their primary method of controlling the public.

Religionists feed off fear and separation by using coercion, criticism, and ridicule, creating fear amongst their flock who fill their coffers in the hope of gaining entrance to heaven. Religionists corrupt the minds of the very young with their dogma, which almost guarantees another generation of contributors to their bank accounts. This is immorality at the highest level—brainwashing the very young before they have reached the age of reason.

Looking at greedy people throughout history, they all seem to die in poverty—the poverty of health that is caused by the love of money.

In some cases, they die of poverty of spirit by committing suicide.

In some cases, they die in the prisons they were sent to by the courts for committing crimes of taking money.

In most cases, they live a walking death, experiencing hell on Earth because they are weak in compassion, and are constantly seeking ways of getting something for nothing.

Greedy people are good at accumulating money but poor in spirit, compassion, and health.

Greedy people are the true definition of small people—people of small-mindedness.

Their only focus is the bottom line, and they don't care how they get it. They usually try to get as much as they can without giving a fair equivalent in use value in return.

Greedy people have a foul demeanour. They are not pleasant to be associated with. They are constantly worried about the bottom line and will chastise, criticize, and ridicule those who spend their money. They have no time for those who cannot help or are unwilling to further their ability to accrue more money.

To the oligarchs, employees are seen as resources to be plundered. They spend no money to nurture or help their people when they are in need.

Greedy people will tithe to their churches to buy their way into heaven. They'll donate to charitable organizations, not because they want to help, but because it makes them look like they are better people than they really are. Appearance is more important to greedy people than the welfare of others.

Greedy people are nasty, hard-headed, and vulgar. Greedy people will fly off the handle at the slightest provocation. Greedy people will fall to pieces, display anger, and hurl insults when faced with challenges and adversity. Greedy people pound their fists on tables and demand results. Greedy people threaten individuals to get results by saying "If you can't do it, I'll find someone who can."

Greedy people try to get something for nothing. They infringe on the rights of others for personal gain, which is the definition of immorality.

This is why being a Nudist or Naturist is so beneficial. You are part of a community that does not criticize or ridicule. A community of acceptance, tolerance, forgiveness, and love. A community that shares what they have and expects nothing in return. A community where people help each other just because they can. A community that co-creates events to be enjoyed and comes up with solutions to challenges that benefit all. A community that promotes individualism and the creation of art. A community that lets people be human beings. We respect each other, and we respect ourselves. We are concerned about the environment and know we are part of the ecosystem. We are responsible human beings and custodians of Mother Earth. Being a Nudist or Naturist is natural.

I love being naked and free, sitting on the grass, connecting with trees, and feeling the sun and the breeze. Fresh air and love are all that I need.

# CHAPTER 6
# Don't Buy Shit

There's a big misconception that we need money and things to be happy. I beg to differ. Yes, we need money to cover our basic needs, but only enough to cover expenses and pay for experiences. We need to be happy in our thoughts before they manifest in reality. The get-rich schemes we create and corrupt our thoughts with are unhealthy. They have never been a good idea. What makes us happy is what we think. We must make ourselves happy on the inside, in our minds, before we can experience comfortable circumstances and environments. We have to work from the inside out.

We've become over-consuming, natural-resource-plundering, Mother Earth-polluting criminals. Yes, I said criminals. When you infringe on the rights of others, and that includes Mother Earth, you are performing immoral, criminal acts. I'm part of the problem.

At least I was for the last six decades because I was taught to think wrong. I perpetuated old archaic ideas.

I've discovered I can get along quite nicely without technology or material wealth, and I only need enough money to meet my basic needs. I've stopped buying shit for instant gratification. I've stopped buying shit to display my net worth. I've stopped buying shit that will last a month or two, and started buying things that will help me prolong my life and look after my body.

I've stopped being a loner and started meeting people with like-minded, Mother Earth-supportive thinking. Instead of buying the next best smartphone, computer, car, or whatever, I'm investing in relationships and creating events people can enjoy and learn from. I'm trying to build a community of people who help each other, not because they want to get paid, but because they want to help. I am creating events that aren't simply entertainment; they're gatherings to come up with solutions to our challenges. They're events that are fun and invigorating. They are events that get people to think and express their creativity. They are events to connect people and find fulfilling ways to live life instead of eking out an existence.

Smartphones and our technology have ripped social interaction away from us. We used to gather in groups to learn from each other, to talk and share experiences and jokes. We've forgotten what it's like to be human. It's in our DNA to socialize. Our technology is a fantastic thing, but I believe it is the most significant contributor to a thing labelled ADHD.

I'm not a physician or a psychologist, but I know that my ability to focus on something has radically diminished over the years. I can sit still for brief periods, but the habit of being entertained and needing to sit in front of an electronic screen seems to be the most important thing to my body. I feel very uncomfortable when I don't get a YouTube fix. It's so bad that when I get overwhelmed at work or need a break for a few minutes, I don't take a break; I pick up the phone and mindlessly surf not-so-social media or Boob Tube instead of reading a book or doing something constructive, like creating an event. Covid has undoubtedly exacerbated the issue. The internet, as great an invention as it is, has been the most significant contributor, in my opinion, to distracted thinking. I think our smartphones, tablets, and laptops are the root cause of ADHD.

I beg parents to get out of the habit of giving infants and toddlers a smartphone to entertain them when they are fussy. Play a game with them. Take them to the park. Tell stories on a long road trip and encourage them to use their creative imagination! Schools will take their ability to imagine beautiful things away soon enough. Parents should encourage creative thinking even if their fantasies appear to be crazy ones. Let them have them, because out of crazy fantasies come great things.

Material things are OK to have, but how much is enough? I know that business owners love to have a lavish life. Wanting toys and to be entertained, they work to make more money for themselves. But what about the human assets that they employ? They're the ones making money for them. How much do they invest in those people? With the current archaic business model, most of them work a J.O.B.—Just Over Broke. Employees barely have enough to meet their needs because the owners, investors, and shareholders need their pockets lined. It's a lousy business model.

You're not necessarily successful if you have a lot of stuff. Material things create an appearance only. I think the most successful people give freely and accept graciously. They are the people I want to hang out with.

Don't buy shit. The novelty will wear thin. The expense of maintaining stuff and appearances will cause stress and possible illness. Help others become wealthy; your wealth has no direction to go but up. When you are naked, you lose the disguises and are being natural. The stress of maintaining an appearance is gone. The joy of helping others emerges. Fulfilment and naked natural existence re-emerge. It's the way we were thousands of years ago, and it can be the same again if we learn to think and love to help each other.

Don't buy shit. Invest in people by creating friendships and connecting to human beings again. Create social events where people can get together and exchange ideas and offer help to those who have challenges in their lives. This is a far better way to spend your hard-earned money. It's better than tithing to a religious institution or some charitable organization.

# CHAPTER 7

# Education vs Schooling

———⌘———

I keep asking myself and others, do you think humans are being humans? I can't see it. I know that evolution has brought us to this point in history, and for reasons I believe to be accurate, we have, over the course of the last century or two and maybe longer, become human doings. We live to work, particularly in North America, instead of just living and being human beings. I live in a relatively small apartment building and know none of my neighbours. People pass each other in the street and hardly ever speak to each other. We quietly judge others and, in the company of friends, will judge others openly. What has become of our species?

I look around, and everyone works at something other than working towards their goals. Do people actually set goals of personal achievement? I see people toiling and suffering, doing something they are good at doing but not doing what they love to do. I see people "hustling" and not caring about whom they are hustling. I see good people obsessed with their bottom line, not seeing what's in front of them or the possibilities they can create. I think we are not behaving the way we should. I see humans being stressed. I see humans being depressed. I see humans being overweight and out of shape. I see people who are thinking too much about their physical bodies and not spending any time developing the six higher mental faculties we have. They are not aware of their spirit. I see humans oppressed and submitting to what society calls "normal behaviour".

Society's "normal" is not normal in any sense. It's conformity. Conformity is the opposite of courage. In some countries, humans are forced to conform to behave the way the authorities want them to, or they are imprisoned or persecuted, and if they speak out against the regime, they may even be murdered. Bravery is to be one's self and be who we are individually. Being a Nudist or Naturist is a step in the right direction; being part of a community that lives peacefully with each other, expressing tolerance, acceptance, forgiveness, and love easily and without thought; co-creating an environment of peace and living without being stressed, not living to work and living to be.

What if we learned to study ourselves? What if we all understood our thoughts and feelings? What if we could take control of our thoughts and direct our energy towards co-creating a beautiful life for ourselves? To be naked and free, just as natural as we are meant to live. Would that not translate to others? Would our actions help others achieve their goals? Wouldn't we experience fulfilling and wonderful rewards if we all learned to think?

An educated person is not necessarily one who has accumulated a vast amount of specialized or general knowledge. An educated person has so developed the faculties of the mind that they can acquire anything they want without infringing on the rights of others. [paraphrased]

—Napoleon Hill, *Think and Grow Rich*, Chapter 5, "Specialized Knowledge"

Napoleon Hill says that controlling one's behaviour is not taught in schools and should be mandatory. Self-control is something anyone can learn. If I can do it, so can anyone.

There are six higher mental faculties that humans have been gifted with. These faculties of the mind are what separates humans from all other species. They are, in no particular order, will, imagination, perception, reason, intuition, and memory. I was utterly ignorant of this fact until I met Bob Proctor. Who was he? He passed away in February 2022, and at that time, he owned twenty-plus companies and was very wealthy. Yes, he wore fine suits and had a nice car and a very modest home in a suburb of Toronto (that I went to after attending several of Bob's seminars called "The Matrixx"). But you wouldn't have known how wealthy he was. He was such a humble and down-to-earth person.

His estate continues to earn revenue, which is funnelled to worthy philanthropic causes. He was the most generous person I have ever met. Bob was a master of his behaviour, and he loved all things and everyone. The last thing he said to me in a personal conversation was "keep studying; it gets easier". He didn't mean to go to school and get another bit of wallpaper. He meant to look inside and find who's there, change the bad habits into good ones, and keep looking to help others. He taught me how to think *big*, and I'm starting to use his lessons to do just that.

There's a big difference between education and schooling. Schooling is what most people confuse with education. Schooling is sitting in a classroom with twenty or thirty other children listening to a well-meaning and excellent teacher drone on about a subject that interests only one or two students. The information being provided is just information. And the children are expected to sit in that classroom and listen. They're forced to pay attention. They're not allowed to use their imagination for daydreaming. They get brainwashed into behaving like everyone else, and ridicule and criticism are used to install these ideas in young fertile minds. The schooling continues in high school—move from classroom to classroom, sit and listen to the information, write essays and quizzes. At the end of the semester, the students are provided with report cards, and for most children, anxiety rises because they have to present that card to their parents. If that report card shows anything below an A, the children often fear the criticism they would receive for not being above-average students.

The report card is used to direct the future of the student. It's supposed to describe what the student is capable of, but it does no such thing. The most erudite scientist could not tell anyone what they are capable of, yet we think that standardized testing can. The only things that a report card states are that a person sat in a classroom on a particular day for a certain length of time and could regurgitate an amount of memorized information in a manner acceptable to the teacher. Schooling is practicing memory. Schooling is an institution of control. No matter how much schooling a person accumulates, schooling is designed to turn people into minions. They are enslaving people to work in factories and businesses, not of their own making but belonging to someone whose mind is firmly set on money and their personal bottom line.

Wouldn't you be outraged if you knew your rights were being infringed upon? Schooling teaches nothing about human rights. Schooling is an institution set up over a hundred years ago, and nothing has changed in the schooling methods since. Schools have not progressed in understanding the mind and the thoughts produced within it or how to inspire students.

At five years old, a person is just beginning to develop their higher mental faculty of reason. But because they are forced to sit quietly in a dark classroom with thirty other children—forced to pay attention to what's on the board; forced to listen to a well-meaning and excellent person lecture on a subject that holds no interest for the child— stress is induced in those children. They are stifling the creative imagination by pushing it to a dark recess of the mind where it atrophies. And then, the children are tortured by being forced to sit in a classroom for a specific amount of time to answer questions presented on paper, requiring them to exercise their memory to be awarded a useless grade.

Please be aware that I understand that schooling is essential. But schooling is not, and never has been, a good way of doing things.

True education teaches people, no matter how old, how their thoughts control their feelings, how their feelings translate into actions, and how their actions accrue the results they experience—teaching people to understand their six higher mental faculties and exercising them to create powerful tools they can use to create the life they wish. Education should be teachers being students and students teaching the teachers. Students could then study what they want to study and excel at becoming whom they want to be. Students would learn that the challenges they face are just challenges they can overcome using their creative imagination. They could focus with their will on the results they want, using their faculty of reason to choose the right direction and make decisions. They could use their perspective to see a different view of where they are going, listen to their intuition and follow their hearts, and wisely use their memory to aid them in not creating the same mistakes repetitively.

All we want as humans is to live in peace and harmony with each other, Nature, and Mother Earth. We want to play and relax and be. We want to be happy and fulfilled. We want to be free. It all starts with an idea and with an understanding of ourselves. Educating people to become consciously aware of their actions, feelings, and, therefore, their thoughts will allow them to behave in a manner that will not infringe on the rights of others.

Nudism is an excellent start to that education. Along with tension and stress goes the posturing and impersonation of someone we are not. We shed our clothes to give great relief to our bodies. We are authentic. There is no judgement or ridicule. There are no harsh words exchanged. There is an exchange of creative ideas. Some of them differ, but that's what being human is all about. It's OK if someone doesn't align with our perspective or ideas, but by having conversations and being open-minded enough to change our mindset and accept when we are wrong, things can only get better. That's what Naturists do best.

Right here, I want to interject my knowledge of our higher mental faculty known as "imagination". What I have been taught through personal development is that we have two types of imagination— the creative imagination and the synthetic imagination. As I stated earlier, the creative imagination is something that our parents and school teachers tell us is just for little children. As children, we have no rules to follow. We freely imagine great things, like pretending to be an astronaut or a police person, a doctor or lawyer, or whatever comes to our fertile imaginings. As toddlers, we played with pots and pans, and who knows what we were imagining.

Then we get schooled with information. The teacher says "Stop daydreaming and looking out the window. Pay attention to what's on the board. That's very important." And our creative imagination gets pushed back into the dark recesses of our minds where it atrophies or gets misused. Our art and talents are set aside as past times, and we're taught that those things cannot earn money for us. The information we gather in school gets placed in our memory and only becomes knowledge if we study the information for an extended period.

The synthetic imagination is something we draw on to create something different, taking some knowledge of one subject and some knowledge from another and combining them in different ways to create something different, not something new.

Our creative imagination is something we can use to create something new. Elon Musk imagines a new world with machines that will sustain human lives on a planet that is inhospitable to human life; he shares that vision with others and inspires them to work with him to reach that goal. That's the correct way to use the creative imagination.

But for the majority of humans, we are taught to use our creative imagination backward. We go through life experiencing good and, what we consider, bad experiences. We live the good experiences without analysing why they are good, and we store the bad experiences in our memory to avoid reliving them. We are trained to use our memory and creative imagination to think about "worst case scenarios" to avoid travelling a path that would lead to disaster. This is the incorrect way to use the creative imagination.

Our dreams can come true. But it takes true faith to live an authentic life. Faith in our abilities and talents. Faith that Mother Earth and Nature will provide everything we need to survive as they have always done since the dawn of time. Using our creative imagination to envision our perfect future is the proper way to use it. Elon is proving this theory correct every day.

Remember that thoughts create feelings, feelings create actions, and actions create results. Consider that if we continuously worry about reliving past experiences and get emotionally involved with these thoughts, our bodies will act on those emotions. Inevitably our results will reflect those thoughts, and the things that we fear end up reoccurring. We are living in the past by using our creative imagination incorrectly.

Imagine, if you will, a world of naked people, happy and genuinely free—no judgements, no criticisms, no worry, no doubts. Imagine that eight billion people accept each other for who and what they are, tolerate each other's perspectives, forgive each other's mistakes, and love each other unconditionally. John Lennon wrote a song called "Imagine". I recommend you listen to it intently. It's a beautiful way to use the creative imagination.

Desire is the key to creating a happy life. I'm not talking about sexual desire, either. Can you imagine where you would be if you dreamed about a perfect future and developed a burning desire to acquire what you want? A burning desire means you are committed to making a change, and you'll burn all bridges behind you to prevent yourself from going in reverse. Just being interested in making changes means you'll only do what's convenient, and changes will come slowly, if at all. Commitment means you will do what is necessary: you want this bright and amazing future life so bad you'd be willing to die in an attempt to achieve it. If you can build your desire for such a result to this level, nothing will stop you from achieving it.

> If I want to be free, I've got to be me.
> Not the me I think you think I should be,
> Not the me I think my wife thinks I should be,
> Not the me I think my kids think I should be,
> If I want to be free, I've got to be me.
> —Bill Gove

Dreams come true.

# CHAPTER 8

# Reprogramming

I n the darkest recesses of the subconscious mind resides the paradigm. The paradigm is a nest of habits that we have accumulated since birth. A habit is an idea or group of ideas we accepted as we grew, and constantly re-accept and reuse as we age.

An example would be that we get up in the morning at the same time; we go to the bathroom and execute our morning rituals there; we grab a cup of coffee and sit down with our breakfast and the newspaper (like anyone reads those anymore) or our smart devices and get caught up on what's happening; we take a picture of our feet and post that on Facebook and then get ready for work. We leave at the same time every day, take the same route to work, punch the clock and start our work, and then go home the same way we came and do the same things we did the day before.

The paradigm lets us execute our actions on autopilot. We can sit in our cars and drive safely to our intended destination and never be present in our minds about what we are doing while operating the vehicle. We can think about all kinds of stuff other than safely driving a weapon of mass destruction. Any driver I have ever spoken to has experienced an incident where they arrived where they were going but did not remember the journey.

That is how most human beings wander this Earth—totally oblivious to the journey and just doing the same things day in and day out, not thinking, just reacting. That is the power of the paradigm.

Now think about all the other habits you think about during your day. If you can identify them, then you are on your way to making changes.

The terrible thing about the paradigm is that it does not like change. It will resist change in the most heinous ways possible. Remember that the paradigm resides in the subconscious mind and enjoys staying hidden and safe there. Become aware of it, and I know an uneasy feeling will befall you as it did me.

When I first started to study personal development, I got involved with a young woman, and I was eager to talk to her about what I was learning. When I told her about the paradigm, she became physically agitated. "I don't like that word," she said, and when I pressed her to find out why, she could not articulate the feeling in words.

What I know now is that what this young woman felt was the paradigm wanting to stay hidden. I was calling it out, and it didn't like it. She and I parted ways shortly after that, so I'm unsure if she overcame her paradigm. I'm sorry that I couldn't help her more.

The paradigm holds ideas like "I'm not worthy of …" and "I can't do that because …" and "I'm not smart enough." These habitual ideas get engrained in us as children, and we carry them with us all of our lives. They become pretty debilitating later in life.

The good news is that the paradigm can be changed. This must be done if someone wants to change their life. This is the work. It's fun and challenging. It's demanding and rewarding. It's the most rewarding work you will ever do.

Every person on the planet has a different vision of what success means. If we want to become more successful, we have to define what that is. Earl Nightingale coined the definition as being the "progressive realization of a worthy ideal". Now the questions arise—what is that worthy ideal in your mind, and how much is enough?

A book is a painting in words. Van Gogh said, "First, I dream my painting, then I paint my dream." Draw a picture of your success in your mind. Then write it out in a journal in as much detail as possible while giving your dream all the love you can. When you write, you're thinking on paper, and that's where a plan begins to materialize.

Your paradigm will give you every excuse you need to stop writing. It'll make you feel anxious and nauseous and fill your mind with ideas like "You're crazy. You'll never make it," or "Everyone will make fun of you." But you will have what you want if you don't listen to those words and push through the anxiety and the voices in your head. And that takes practice. You'll have to fight your paradigm every day until it changes. It takes no less than thirty days of constant repetition of new ideas to replace old bad ideas in your paradigm. So keep reading your painting and keep writing! The more excited you get about your ideas, the faster your ideas will come to life.

Some of your older programs will need some extra effort to override. The longer you've practiced the old negative thoughts, the stronger your paradigm will hold onto them. You can only change one or two habits at a time, so choose your battles wisely.

Bob, if you could work with him, would give you an exercise to determine what habits need to be broken. He'd have you list all the negative results you're experiencing and then write out the polar opposite of those results on a clean sheet of paper. Then you'd pick the most exciting new result you listed and repeat that for no less than thirty days.

I have built a fantasy. I won't go into it here, but it's an imaginary picture of how I want my world to be. It's my image, and I continuously try to keep it in my mind. I know whom I must become to make this image manifest, and I try with all my will to be that person. Remember that the will is one of our six higher mental faculties. I exercise my will by doing this, and it strengthens daily.

I fail at trying a lot, but I return to being who I want to be as much as possible. I see how I must behave when interacting with people, and try to be like that all day. When I catch myself behaving in a way that doesn't match how I want to act, I know that my old programming caused me to behave that way.

Some people have told me "You live in a fantasy world, and you'll be disappointed when it doesn't work out that way." This is what schooling does to us. We're told that fantasizing is just for small children. We have to stop being children and start adulting at an early age. We must learn lessons that will carry us "*safely*" through life and live by those rules, boundaries, and limitations.

I hate to say this, but that's what makes us sick. When we try to be someone we're not, we constantly try to meet the expectations we *think* others want us to meet. That is mind pollution of the worst kind. We get caught up in being selfish. We worry more about our appearances and how to get something for nothing. We don't look at the bigger picture, and never discover the hidden talent within us until it's too late.

Nudism is a relief to the mundane. When I shed my clothes, I no longer try to be who *everyone else expects* me to be. I'm being authentic and genuine. There are no pretences, and I'm not projecting an image of who I am not. I am being as real as I am, exposed to the world, transparent and free. Liberation!

When we get tired of the daily grind and ask empowering questions like "How can I use my talents and abilities to serve others?", we go from being selfish to being selfless. Next thing you know, our worlds are expanding, our daily efforts take us closer to our goals, and our fantasies soon become a reality.

Fantasize. Dream big, bold, beautiful dreams about how you want your corner of the world to be. You're allowed to do that. You don't need anyone's permission to do it. Build your fantasy. Get emotionally involved with it. Write down a plan to execute and then take action. Let your emotions propel you forward, and let your intuition guide you. It'll never steer you wrong.

Dream big!

# CHAPTER 9

# The Health of the Human Body

———◦∿◦———

Yup! I own one—a body. Sadly, I've abused it all my life. I never realized how important a thing it is. In my youth, I drank and ate all kinds of things. I smoked tobacco and cannabis. I got drunk. Stupidly drunk. I did all sorts of damage to my body by doing what everyone around me did; by being a sheep—following the crowd and trying to fit in.

Halfway through my life, I was fat, brain-dead, depressed, and alone. The mental noise between my ears was deafening. I was seriously contemplating how to off myself painlessly. But of course, that's impossible. I was eating far too much processed junk and fast food. I was not interacting with people—even people in my own family. I had abused my body so much that it was now in a perpetual cycle of self-abuse. I had formed a nasty habit.

My life changed when I became aware of Bob Proctor. It was 7 September 2013. I made a decision based on my intuition, and I started to study with Bob. I became aware that there was something in me that I needed to express; something big that was trying to get out. I realized I had wasted 50 per cent of my life being sick and tired, and started yearning to make changes.

I knew then that I needed to look after my body better. At that time, I was labouring at a sedate job, pushing a mouse around my desktop, and not exercising. My cholesterol and glucose levels were elevated. I was physically sick. I knew that if I wanted to manifest the new life I desired, it would take a while and that I needed to transform my body to live long enough to experience it.

The first thing that had to happen was that I had to start to love my body. I had to change the negative bullshit I thought about my body and create an image in my mind of how I wanted it to be. I wrote it out in a journal. I described what I wanted in great detail and got very emotionally involved with the change. I read that description every day. I added to it in writing. I started to love my body and all of its gifts to me.

I started a new habit of waking up in the morning—as I moved from the bedroom to the bathroom, I'd stop by the mirror in the hallway and look at my naked body and thank it. I thanked it for being healthy and physically attractive. I thanked it for being 165 pounds of perfectly healthy, handsome, and sexy man. I admired it and felt gratitude for it. I thanked it for all its senses and for allowing me to be consciously aware of the sensations it delivered and aware of the world surrounding me. I felt, and still do feel, blessed for my body.

Now, remember that this was 2013. I weighed close to 220 pounds. My stomach was so big I couldn't see my penis without lifting it out of the way. My friends from the southern US told me once that I was suffering from Dunlop Disease. They told me that Dunlop Disease is when your belly "done lopped" over your belt, and you can't see your toes. When you hear that kind of stuff, take it as a warning.

So I saw a body in the mirror that was opposite to the image in my mind. My paradigm was screaming at me "Ha, ha, ha! What a load of shit. You're too lazy to make your body like that. You're a shithead!" and I'd continue on my way. But no matter how hard the paradigm tried to keep things the same, I kept doing that new morning ritual. After a time—and to be honest, I didn't document it well—things started to change.

I'd look at the potato-chip bag as I reached for it and ask "Do I really want this in my body?" Potato chips are a real poison for the body, by the way. I started to ask "Do I really want that greasy, fast-food burger? Or do I want to make something better for my body at home?"

If you look in my cupboards and fridge now, you won't find snack foods. You won't find processed foods. You won't find much but fresh fruits, vegetables, nuts, berries, eggs, and meat. Healthy stuff. I also learned how to eat these wholesome foods. The order of eating them is just as crucial to health as what is eaten. Read *Glucose Revolution* by Jessie Inchauspé to learn what I did.

After several months of these practices, I soon released all but 165 pounds of mass, and my belly got flatter. I started to notice the changes and became more grateful for my body. My cholesterol and glucose were still elevated, but that was from living with stress all my life. Conventional wisdom teaches that elevated cholesterol and glucose are genetic, and I'm here as proof positive it is not. It has to do with stress. The stress hormones wreak havoc on the body at the cellular level. The stupidness of it was that the stress was self-inflicted pressure from my negative thought habits. I would use food to relieve stress or as comfort food. I ate to still the overactive mental noise.

To remedy this, I changed my thoughts. I created goals to achieve and work towards. My energy levels increased. Bob told me, "If you have no energy, you have no desire." I desired change in my body and my life. My energy returned.

I went back to doing more physical work too. I hate going to the gym, so what better way to strengthen a body than to work in a physically active occupation? My cardio needed to increase so that I could help to control my high cholesterol and glucose, so I bought a nice bike. I commute two or three times a week on it. I ride it for thirty to sixty minutes every day, weather permitting, mind you. Without me setting the goal of getting healthier, that bike would have sat in a corner and become a clothes hanger like other exercise equipment I've had.

All of these changes came without effort except for the exercise of looking at my naked body in a mirror and giving it thanks. Nudity is a healthier practice than covering the body in cloth. It's healthier physically, mentally, and spiritually.

Now I do everything in moderation. I only drink alcohol when I'm in a creative mood. It's one glass, and I nurse it for hours. I enjoy the flavour instead of downing it to get drunk. I *never* smoke anything. I'll have some fast food once a week.

From what I recall of my high-school learning, and what I believe to be true, is that over the past ten thousand years, human physiology has not changed that much. Ten thousand years ago, we drank water. We walked everywhere we went, probably naked. We didn't toil. We played at living life naked. We practiced our skills and created safe, friendly, loving nude communities. We only suffered stress when we were being chased by something. We were at peace. Naked, free, and happy. Sex was something we enjoyed and that satiated a physical urge. We didn't get aroused by a thought; we got involved in the activity. The by-product was procreation.

But today, we walk nowhere. We are forced by archaic thinking and human-rights-infringing laws to wear clothes that make us unwell. We don't even walk across the road to the corner store. We drive to the store, schools, and the gym; if we could, we'd drive to the toilet. We sit behind computer monitors, and the most exercise we get is pushing a mouse around the desktop.

We overindulge in what we eat and drink. Sugar is the most dangerous substance we consume, and it is in *everything*. Some people will drink a gallon of coffee in a day. Some will drink several soda pops in a day. Some will eat candy like there's no tomorrow. Some people will have a bottle of wine with dinner and maybe one or two more bottles in the evening. Ask me how I know this.

We suck on vapes and inhale all kinds of chemicals, and *none of it is supposed to be in our lungs*! We inhale tobacco smoke because we think it's calming. We inhale cannabis and other intoxicating drugs to get high—advertisers entice us to do so.

Our lungs were designed to breathe air, use the life-giving elements we inhale, and expel the life-threatening elements we generate as waste. Have you ever wondered why we want to cough when we inhale something we're not supposed to? That's our body telling us to *stop*!

Why do we feel sick if we ingest too much alcohol? It's because alcohol isn't something we are supposed to ingest. It makes a lot of sense to me now that I'm a reformed substance abuser. Please don't make the same mistakes I did when I was young and ignorant. My body is paying for it now.

Everything that we do in excess decreases our life span. We could live much longer if we treated our bodies like the magnificent machines they are.

Many people scoff at this idea. They know their parents and grandparents lived for a certain period and expect they will not live much longer because it's "genetic". I can tell you for sure that this idea is total bullshit. How you treat your body with the types of food you consume and your mental state determines your longevity.

Now, looking after this body I reside in is one of my most important goals. I'm not ready to die yet. I know I will, and I'm not afraid to die, but I have a shit ton more work to do before I transition to the next phase of my eternal journey. I'll be damned if I'm going to let ill health and negative thinking consume my miraculous body. Gratitude is the highest emotional vibration we can place our bodies in. If we are grateful and feel the emotion of gratitude towards our bodies, the body must respond to that vibration. If you have a grateful vibe in your body, every cell will react to that vibe.

Looking after my body hasn't been as difficult a thing as I thought it might be several years ago. It's fun and rewarding knowing I've done something good for it. Having changed to a more positive mindset, I think, is the root of the transformation. Without changing that, there was no hope for a healthier body.

I talked about the paradigm in the last chapter, but here I want to talk about how the paradigm controls our mindset. We get into habitual ways of thinking. I know that when I sit behind the wheel of my car, I'm setting myself up to see all the irritating behaviours of my fellow drivers and how they are hindering traffic flow and *my* progress (selfish). I get very critical, and my criticisms bring up negative emotions. Anger, impatience, hurry, and disgust are all my feelings in a simple fifteen-minute commute.

How did my mindset develop like this? It's simple. Before I started thinking, I sat in a car that one of my parents or grandparents was driving, and I'd hear them criticize the other drivers. I thought that's how you were supposed to operate a car. You were supposed to see all the flawed driving everyone else was doing, and of course, you were doing it perfectly. So having this mindset unknowingly installed in my paradigm, it springs to life without me thinking about it. It's just my reactions to other drivers.

When I scoop my keys off the counter in the morning to head off to work, the dread I feel knowing I have to face Toronto traffic starts those negative emotions at work. Now imagine what my body is experiencing when I feel those emotions. Then I do this daily. What better way to reinforce old habits than to repeat them continuously? After fifty years of doing this, how hard would it be to change that habit? Ten years of concentrated effort in changing it has finally decreased the stress I issue to my body. But I still do it in minor ways, and when I hear myself criticizing, I recognize that I'm practicing an old habit stuck in my paradigm. I apologize to my body for the impatience and ask it for forgiveness.

Now, I have eleven billion habits. I can't change all of them at once. But by strategically placing new thoughts in my mind on a consistent, spaced, repetitive basis, I can change the most important habits, and many of the lesser ones change automatically. Just like the habit of looking at myself and my body in the mirror first thing in the morning and saying "Damn! Look at that hot, sexy, handsome, and perfectly healthy body! I'm so grateful for how it looks and for it carrying me all these years!" even when I was fat and sick, my mindset started to change, and my body morphed and changed. I started feeling healthier and happier. Now I feel more energetic and able to go for longer distances and times. I'm excited about living now, and want to do more for others.

Constant, spaced repetition of a new ideas changes the paradigm. If I place in my mind the ideas of how materially wealthy I want to be and how much is enough, and I constantly repeat these ideas, how long will it take me to manifest them in reality? Nothing will change unless I believe with all my heart that I can achieve what I want and get emotionally involved with the dream. Getting emotionally involved means that you'll drive your body to take action towards manifesting it. To create the belief that I can accomplish anything, I have to repeat that idea over and over again until I truly believe it—just like I did while trying to transform my body.

I succeeded.

# CHAPTER 10

# Men Don't Think

A nd yes, women know we don't think too. It's not something we can hide. But it's something we can change.

I can make that statement because in my younger years (and like most men) I didn't think I could control my erections. "They just happen, man!" I suffered severely during puberty. I was walking around the halls of my high school, a raging hormone on two legs, trying to hide my fully erect penis in my pants behind the notebooks I was carrying. I was so afraid that someone would make fun of me (fear of criticism) or beat me up if they saw I was aroused. But, because of how I carried my books, I drew attention to it. I still got beaten up.

I couldn't understand why erections just came along. It was frustrating and infuriating at times. "Oh, shit! This couldn't have happened at a worse time." It was something that happened to me. I didn't create it.

But now I see that my thoughts indeed caused the erection to manifest. I saw the lace of a bra exposed under the collar of a gorgeous girl's blouse, and that was enough to arouse me.

Because of what I've learned during my personal development, I can tell you that the body will not execute any action unless an emotion is attached to a thought. Emotions drive the body. If I have a thought of anger, my body expresses it with angry actions. If I have thoughts of love and I feel like I'm in love, my body will express that too. If I feel sexy and attracted to someone, my horniness is made apparent.

Thoughts create feelings, feelings create actions, and actions create results. I've said it before, and it works for erections too.

Here's a play-by-play: I see the lacy bra of this beautiful girl appear past the collar of the blouse she's wearing. The thought of interacting with her sexually races through my mind so fast that I have no hope of being aware of it. The conscious thought is simply "oh my god", but unconsciously images of sex flash through the mind. I would get emotionally involved with these thoughts, and my body responded by producing the erection. At that age, I wasn't aware of how to be aware. I'd never been taught about conscious awareness in school. I hadn't learned it from my parents or other authoritative people. I reacted to my circumstance, and because of my ignorance in knowing how to control my thoughts, my penis would pop up, and anxiety followed closely behind it. Because of my ignorance, I couldn't say "Hang on a second. That's not a good thought to have. It's a pleasant one but not an appropriate time or place for it." I would have been better equipped to stop the erection from forming if I'd known then what I know now. Hindsight, after all, is twenty-twenty.

The other problem was that I grew up in a textile household. I was taught that nudity was for bathing and sex, and sex couldn't be had if you weren't married (and for any purpose other than procreation). In other words, nudity was not permitted outside the bathroom or bedroom. It was considered sinful if I appeared naked at any other time. That caused stress in the mind of a young person.

If I had grown up in an open home where nudism was practiced, I would not have sexualized that pretty girl for wearing a frilly bra. I would have been more aware of the person than the body the person owned. Chances are, I wouldn't have gotten aroused at all. Growing up in a Nudist family, I would not have sought images of naked girls or women in adult magazines. It would not have been an issue, because I would have grown up around naked girls and boys. The titillation of seeing a naked woman would not exist, because nudity would have been normal for me.

Most men will be victims of sensual feedback and become aware of the sensations their erect penises in their pants are sending them. They make no effort to change their thoughts because the sensations they receive from their erect penises are very pleasurable. Non-thinking men will have more sexual thoughts and entertain them instead of controlling them and seeking ways to release the built-up tension in them. "I can't control my penis" they will say, and they just let it happen.

Awareness of the emotion causing the erection would have been a benefit way back then. I could have said, "Wait a second, why am I horny?" That's how I control it now. I have the thought, but before my penis takes over, I dismiss the idea, giggle, and move forward with my day. I change my thoughts and redirect my sexual energy towards action on my goal. It's the "horniness" sensation that makes me aware of what I'm thinking. It's pretty funny when I think about it. If I didn't know how my mind and body are connected, I might lose control of my thoughts, continue being horny, and continue to entertain my erection. There's a time and place to engage in these thoughts, like when I'm involved in sexual activity.

Napoleon Hill wrote a complete chapter, number eleven, on "The Mystery of Sex Transmutation" in his book *Think and Grow Rich*. It describes changing what he called the emotion of sex into an effort to achieve a goal. He stated, and I paraphrase here, that the emotion of sex is the most potent emotion available to humans. I cannot disagree with that. But I think sex is more of an urge than an emotion. Think about how much energy it takes to create a baby and how fast you could achieve a goal if you diverted that much energy from the act of sex to action towards your goal.

Knowing how to control my emotions has been invaluable to keeping the peace and finding a solution to conflict instead of escalating negative emotions. It's the same way with any emotional state. If I get angry because someone successfully pressed one or more of my buttons, I can stop and say "Don't get emotionally involved in this; it's not worth it." To me, anger is stupidity manifested. Most men, unfortunately—and I was one of them—would fly off the handle and lash out at the person who pushed the buttons, escalating the situation and possibly having it end in violence and assault charges, or broken relationships and lack of trust.

Keep in mind that women can behave similarly. I have been at the brunt of an abusive relationship too.

Most men hide their compassion and empathy because they are taught that showing emotions is not *manly*. Yes, I was a victim of this inhumane mental construct. Men stuff themselves into pigeonholes that were made for them by stupid men generations previously. They unknowingly bottle up their feelings, and the body pays the price. I am the poster child of that concept and the vial concepts of the Brocode. I will get backlash from all the manly men who might read this. But I'm prepared to counter that with compassion and empathy.

I know being vulnerable and expressing sensitive emotions is *more* manly. It takes *balls* to show your authenticity, like it takes courage to break away from conforming to social norms and be naked in a community. You're healthier for it when you show compassion and express empathy. By doing so, you connect with others on a visceral level. There are so many musicians and singers that reach their audiences by pouring their emotions into their songs. Men can learn from this.

What I found from being a Nudist is that I get to be authentic. If I get moved by a stunning performance of music, acting, or a beautiful painting or work of art, I get to be real and let my emotions show. No one criticizes. No one ridicules. When I shed my clothes, it is liberating. I'm no longer trying to fit into a pigeonhole forced upon me by a narrow-minded culture or people. I'm not inhibited by trying to follow the unwritten rules of the Bro-code, and I get to express who I am and display what I am feeling without fear of criticism. I can control the circumstance that would place me in the way of criticism because I know how to think.

There is great consternation in society today about gender identification. It seems to me that there have been no scientific studies on the subject and, therefore, no empirical evidence that can be presented to support either perspective. Some believe gender identity is a mental illness, and some believe that gender fluidity is an actual mental construct.

I find that religion plays a big part in addressing this issue. Religious people are more apt to label, criticize, and ridicule people into behaving like what is written in their archaic thinking scriptures. This causes resistance from those who support gender-questioning individuals. It has become a legal battle, and I feel that far too much time has been spent on the debate. If we all accept that there are eight billion people on Mother Earth and no two think exactly alike, does it not make sense to stop trying to fit in and just be who we are authentically? Without shame or remorse. Without apology. Does it not make sense then to practice acceptance and tolerance? Is that not the essence of being human? Isn't it time we just say "Fuck it! Live and let live."?

There is a caveat to my statements above. I support the idea that everyone is allowed to believe what they will. Still, I am concerned with the health of people who would undergo surgery to transform into the physical being they identify as. Our bodies are miracles, and if we have the misfortune to be born into a body that is not what we identify as, it makes no sense to mutilate the magnificent, perfect human body to transform it. People need to practice acceptance and be at peace with their physical form. Being at peace is what human beings are meant to experience. Decide who and what you are, and make a stand as such. Be proud but not obnoxious. Be confident but not conceited.

Learning how to think shifts the focus from ourselves and our needs to how to be selfless and help others be successful. Being authentic and vulnerable is liberating and healthy. When you learn to make that change in perspective, magic happens.

# CHAPTER 11
# Sex in the Naturist World

I don't think any writing on Nudism and Naturism would be complete without discussing sex. I don't know about you, but I like sex. I have, what I consider, physical urges to experience an orgasm. I call it a biological urge because I believe the body must express it to be healthy. Being a Nudist taught me that I can control my sexual behaviour.

As stated in a previous chapter, most people don't understand this concept. Most people are controlled by our textile society and the rules of nudity. If you were to go to a Nudist or Naturist park, you'd be able to see that people do control their sexual behaviour. I've been to "adult parks" and am a member of Bare Oaks Family Naturist Park. I find the atmosphere at Bare Oaks more relaxing, and people are more inclined to accept single male members than in adult parks.

Like any culture, there are rules that members are expected to follow. At my park, open sexual activity is strictly prohibited. But what occurs in the privacy of your trailer, mobile home, park model home, camping tent, or rented room is perfectly acceptable. My park prohibits talk about sex in the proximity of vulnerable people, and that's just common sense, in my opinion.

We are human and prefer having privacy when engaging in sexual activities. Please don't misunderstand me—hugs, kissing, and displays of affection are allowed. But heavy petting and passionate kissing are not conducive to a comfortable and non-sexual environment.

Here's a simple set of rules that I follow, which relieve me of a great deal of stress. Pick a place and time where sexual activity is appropriate. In social gatherings, confine your conversation to helping humanity and each other. When discussing sex, don't get into vivid descriptions of fantasies and avoid those people who do nothing but talk about those.

When I feel the urge to experience an orgasm, I have two choices. The first is to satiate the appetite by expressing it physically at a time and in a place that is appropriate for such activity, and the second is to redirect it into action towards my goal. In other words, I direct my energy instead of letting it control me. Which do you think I prefer?

It takes conscious thinking. It takes conscious awareness of our emotional state to be able to redirect our energy and stay in a state of being relaxed and easy-going. Yes we will react to our circumstances, and when we become aware that we are about to react, we can consciously look at our emotions and say "I need to change what I'm thinking." Doing this teaches us to respond to our circumstances instead of reacting. People will naturally gravitate towards you if you deal with your circumstances in this manner. When a sexual thought occurs, one can adjust their thinking to manage their behaviour. Thoughts create feelings, feelings create actions, and actions create results.

Sex is fun and should be engaged in, but it's essential to control the urges and to be mindful of one's situation. Doing so allows one to be free. It allows us to express our sexuality without guilt or fear of being shamed. It allows us to be human beings. Teaching teenagers the same skills is essential to good health.

Anything goes. Your wildest fantasies can be experienced. Being honest and brave enough to make them happen is what it takes, and it's all OK. To be free, you cannot be afraid of criticism or ridicule. Just be you.

In a committed relationship, being open and honest about your desires and making them known to your spouse takes courage. Communication is critical, and being free from fear of criticism and ridicule makes it easy to talk about your fantasies. If you're on the receiving end of listening to your spouse's desires, you may not like them at first, but giving yourself time to consider them and make an adult decision will give your relationship some deep connection.

As I stated before, an orgasm is what we are after when we engage in sexual activity. But there's a real possibility of creating life by performing the activity. Are you prepared for that? If procreation is the goal of the activity, why are you bringing this new human being into the world? Is it just because your parents had babies, and they're pressuring you into getting them a grandchild? That's not a good reason.

Are you bringing this new human into the world to make it a better place? What are you willing to sacrifice to help that human succeed in whatever purpose it gives itself? Will you program it according to what you were programmed with? Or will you give it all the resources it needs and all of your time to give that new human being the power to be *awesome*?

Life is a journey; if you're not prepared to place your child on a path of success, you should re-evaluate your decision to procreate.

# CHAPTER 12

# Helping Others

The most fulfilling thing in a human endeavour is helping others. Let's face facts: it feels great to be of service to others and know that you've made a difference.

I was once told that we all want to be important. I'm afraid I have to disagree. I think we all want to be fulfilled by impacting humanity with our lives. Not everyone wants fame or fortune. Most people want peace, tranquillity, and fulfilment.

We've created this culture that programs us to believe that money is the most important thing we can labour to get. Money is essential, but would you not agree that living life is more important?

What do you like to do? What are you really good at doing? What fulfils you? How can you use your talents and abilities to benefit humanity?

We live in a world where our various cultures have made minions out of human beings. We toil to acquire money to pay bills. This is not a sustainable system, as we see from various countries' economic situations. They have one thing in common: the debt they are in. Our greed and lust for material wealth require hoarding money and accumulating things. Money needs to flow to be effective in making a change or being of benefit to humanity. But the hoarding of money and material things bring about strife. Money is essential, but more important is living in peace.

The novelty of owning things soon disappears, and we are now toiling to maintain those things. When we get tired of those things, they end up in a landfill or sold to the next person that will work at keeping it until it no longer functions or they grow weary of maintaining it and, again, it ends up in a landfill.

The last thing on our minds is helping others be successful. If we start a business, we usually start it to replace our income. We work the business until it grows to a point where it generates enough money to meet our basic needs, and we find that we can only do so much work. Complacency sets in. We may hire some people to do the work we don't want to do, but we find that the administration of employees is complicated.

If the company grows beyond a certain number of employees and we find it increasingly more challenging to deal with them, we'll cut back the company until we feel it's manageable. With employees on board, we get narrowly focused on income because now we have to worry about generating enough income to meet the basic needs of the employees. We watch the bottom line and work to keep the company in the black. We soon lose the excitement of owning a company. We never imagine how big and beautiful an entity we could make the organization.

Soon we run into saturation. We can only perform so well for so long. Our enthusiasm decreases, and the burden of responsibility weighs heavy on our shoulders. The employees and customers feel it, and the bottom line reflects it. We have become business operators instead of business owners.

What's the difference? An operator will work their life away, toiling to keep the company afloat. An operator will go out and actually do the work. And they'll do the bookkeeping, and they'll do sales, and they'll do whatever task needs to be done, including cleaning the bathroom if no one else will do it for them. They'll micromanage work for the employees instead of trusting them to do it unsupervised.

On the other hand, a business owner inspires people to come and work with them. An owner will create an image of what they want the business to look like and co-create solutions to manifest the big vision with their co-workers, following an organized and co-created plan. They allow their co-workers to use their talents and abilities to achieve that goal, making their work fulfilling. They encourage making mistakes and learning from them. They encourage creativity, and help them create solutions to the challenges they face. Not just the challenges of the business but personal challenges as well.

Can you imagine what an employee would feel like working in a company with such an inspiring owner? Do you think the employees would be happy and love coming to work to find fulfilment and want to be there to help each other? How would the company's customers feel when dealing with cheerful and helpful employees? Do you think repeat business is likely? How would the bottom line look for a company like this? How will investors or shareholders benefit? Win-win-win.

An owner will focus on the outcomes they want. They will be in control of their emotions. They will have a calm and collected demeanour and be poised in the face of adversity. They will find lessons in failures, and continuously move towards the big goals while trying to be a better person today than they were yesterday.

The current business model taught in most colleges and universities is based on archaic principles that narrowly focus on profits and placate investors' and shareholders' avarice. "We want 10 per cent more return on our investment every quarter." Greed. Presidents of companies are now pressured to make that unrealistic demand manifest. The pressure is passed from the top ranks right through a company to the lowest-paid, part-time employees. Miserable employees do not interact with customers well. When customers experience negative vibrations, words, and actions, they soon look for alternative suppliers for their business.

Co-creative companies focus on the employee's well-being. They pay their employees handsomely for their efforts because their bottom line demands it. When co-creative employees feel valued and an intrinsic part of an organization, they are happier, healthier, and more willing to do a little extra for others. I don't mean working longer hours or working harder. I mean being more attentive to what they are doing and less likely to waste time bitching and moaning. A positive environment leads to positive customer interaction, which leads to repeat business and, therefore, a better bottom line and happier investors and shareholders.

If we could turn our cultures away from selfish endeavours to be materially wealthy and move towards being spiritually, physically, and intellectually rich, our cultures would benefit. Finding an inspirational leader who would co-create changes instead of pandering to lobbyists, oligarchs, religionists, or a vocal minority would be challenging. But by doing so, our cultures, as varied and diverse as they are, would be able to live in harmony.

What has to change? We need to educate our children. We need them to understand that accumulating vast amounts of money should not be their goal. We must get them on the path of supporting and nurturing Mother Earth and reconnecting to Nature. We must teach them to co-create instead of striving for material wealth and stature. Sustaining human life on Mother Earth is what we need to figure out, and by teaching our children that there are no differences between people—that if we look at the person instead of the body, or the culture, or the region of the world they are from, or the beliefs, or even the colour of their skin—we can live in harmony, helping each other not just to survive but to thrive.

We must teach them to set goals and stop being meandering wanderers. We need to show them how to create a plan to achieve their goals and support them 100 per cent, no matter how outrageous we think their ideas are. We need to teach them how to determine how much is enough. Remember that children did not ask to be brought into this world, so we owe them *everything* to help them be successful, naked (if they choose to be so), shameless (because that is their birthright), and free.

We need to teach our children about values—tolerance, acceptance, forgiveness, and love. We must teach them that expressing compassion and empathy are good things and that all challenges are solved by giving freely and accepting graciously. We should help our children understand the incredible power within them to do what they love, and direct their efforts towards helping each other thrive. To stand up for their principles and live life instead of living to work.

We need to stop trading and start giving. Expecting compensation for doing what we love to do from the person we are doing it for is merely survival. But if we do what we love to do for anyone who wants what we do, we thrive, and our compensation will emerge from sources we cannot imagine would compensate us.

We need to start behaving like human beings again.

# CHAPTER 13

# Enough Already

———ᏧᏏ———

O K, OK. You've made it this far, and I thank you for sticking it out. I hope I've opened your eyes to some things, and I hope I've inspired you to study yourself. If you can understand why you behave how you do, and if you can understand that you can indeed morph into the person you want to be, you can understand everyone and help them achieve their greatness while achieving yours.

Having this awareness leads to success. Meeting people with excitement, compassion, empathy, and a desire to be selfless while doing what you love must lead you to more incredible things. The ability to be vulnerable and open is true freedom. Nudity is the physical expression of vulnerability and is unbelievably liberating. Being authentic and free to express what's inside you is the healthiest way to live. You'll be safe in a Naturist or Nude community.

What's your vision? I implore you to sit down in a place where distractions are limited and turn off your phone. Don't just set it on silent mode—*turn it off.* Turn off your computer, TV, and radio; kick your spouse and kids out and be with yourself. Get into a really relaxed state and let calmness invade your overwhelmed mind for no less than forty-five minutes. Then write for fifteen minutes about what you want. Is one hour a day for yourself so hard to give up? Bob said to make a shopping list of wants. From that list, you'll find one thing to move on—something you want to go after; something that moves you emotionally; something that excites you.

What are you outraged by? What or who inspires you? Can you move a cause forward? What do you love to do?

When you write, you have to think. When you write, you're thinking on paper. Write it all out.

What service could you provide to benefit others?

What product could you produce to provide to others?

What talents do you have? What do you love doing?

> First, I dream my painting, and then I paint my dream.
> —Vincent Van Gogh

I know one or two very talented musicians. They could make a lot of money, but they believe that they're not good enough and that it is too hard to earn a living playing music. (I wonder if Pink feels that way.) With an attitude like this, a vision is nearly impossible to develop. Somewhere along their journey, they met with a negative idea about playing their instrument or singing that stopped them from moving forward. It was likely an idea that wasn't theirs.

Their belief is partly due to them starting a family before they started earning money from playing. Then they got caught in the "I have to provide for them" trap. They are totally unconscious thinkers who are ignorant of who they are. One is a classically trained musician. She tries very hard to play the music as it is written on the score sheet. It's technically correct, but it seems like she doesn't feel the music. That shows when she plays. It's a shame really. People don't get moved by her performance because she isn't moved by it either. She's emotionally disconnected from her performance.

On the other hand, Pink is emotionally connected to her singing and dancing. She doesn't have to be technically correct; she fucks up singing all the time, yet she keeps singing. She pours emotion into her performances, which allows her to connect with her audience. She has a vast audience. The only thing that Pink worries about is how to be better in her next show.

The last thing that she worries about is what others think about her. She gets out there, says what she believes is true, and feels sorry for those who criticize her. She has a vision of what she wants, and she gets rewarded for providing her art of entertainment. She is emotionally involved with her vision.

That's how excited and emotionally involved I beg you to get with your writing. Look at your list. Find the one thing you want more than anything else. Now make a plan to achieve it. Fall in love with the good you are doing.

Stand up for your principles. When you do that, you'll always succeed.

The short-term goals should be moving you towards your big picture. This book is a small step towards my goal. It's small steps that lead to massive success.

Fear is something that you will encounter. But understand that fear is the child of worry and doubt and manifests itself as anxiety on the physical plane. Worry and doubt are mental dis-eases. There's no reason for worry or doubt, but you have to learn to believe that.

The biggest hurdle to success is overcoming fear. Thoughts create feelings. Feelings create actions. Actions create results. Feelings of anxiety often stop people from taking a step. But when you become aware that anxiety and excitement are the same feeling but with different polarities, you can instantly realize that if you push past the anxiety, you will grow by taking the step you're hesitating on. You become excited knowing that you will succeed by taking the step. The first step is the hardest.

It's the start that stops most people.

—Don Shula

There's a secret to success that really isn't that secret. Bob taught me this, and all credit goes to him and the mentors he's had. To be more successful, look at who is in your sphere of influence. Are they successful? Finding a group of people who are like-minded and have similar interests as you to hang out with is very important. Here's the trick to it. I was taught to create what's known as a Master Mind. It's a group of two or more people who want to help each other. This group should meet several times a week to discuss wants and provide whatever assistance members need. The meeting should be limited to a maximum of eight people, but if there are more people in your Master Mind group, start a second Master Mind.

Before the meeting, there can be social interaction. But the discussion needs to be businesslike. The social aspect should be free of adult intoxicants like alcohol and other substances. It starts at the same time on the same day of the week every week, punctually. The session lasts no more than sixty minutes. A moderator and a note taker are selected. Each member is given a specific amount of time to speak. The hour should be divided evenly among the members, and the moderator should choose the order of the speakers. Each member gets to describe their wins and wants; others should listen intently. If an attending member knows they can help the speaker with their want, they'll raise their hand, and the note taker writes down who wants to assist which speaker.

After the hour, all members are welcome to stay and socialize some more. Those that said they could help someone have an opportunity to set up a private meeting on another day with the person they want to support.

Everyone in a Master Mind should be willing to drop whatever they are doing and attend a meeting whenever another member calls for one. But the calling member should be ready to arrange a convenient time for those they called upon.

Don't forget that no one is willing to give endlessly. You must be willing to give freely without expectation of rewards for your effort. All members are there to help *each other.*

In a Master Mind, goals are discussed. Be very careful not to steal the dream of any of the members. You may know how to do what another member needs help with, but taking their idea and making it work for you would be unethical. If you know how to do something another member wants to do, it's up to you to teach the member in need—that's fair and equitable. Your rewards will come to you from other sources.

I know you may be wondering "Why call it a Master Mind?" The answer is powerful, and I will do my best to describe it.

When two people gather together and start sharing positive ideas to achieve a goal, magic happens. The positive ideas generate more positive ideas. It's like a third mind enters the association. Positive ideas beget more positive ideas. Solutions for challenges happen. You've been part of a Master Mind already. You've sought help from a manager or supervisor for a challenge you were facing, and together you came up with a solution or found someone else who could help. It was informal, but a Master Mind nonetheless.

Now think of seven people you trust, and discuss creating this Master Mind group.

# CHAPTER 14

# Tying It All Together

———◦◦◦———

Y ou've read a lot in this short book. I tried to keep it concise, short, and sweet so you could make the best of it. The steps to being naked, shameless, human, and free are simple. Follow these instructions, and freedom is right around the corner. A problem arises when you only read this once—you'll have the essential information you need to succeed, but you'll have a hard time succeeding, because you haven't turned the information into knowledge. Read this chapter every day. It's not a long read. Then act on what you've learned.

Decide to liberate yourself.

Create a goal. Make it an outrageous goal—something big, bold, and beautiful (B³); something you've never done before. Make it something you want so desperately you'd be willing to die trying to get it and, simultaneously, that will scare the hell out of you.

Write it out. Write out your goal in the most incredible detail possible. What does it feel like to achieve it? What does it look like? What does it smell like? What does it sound like? What does it taste like? What do you physically feel when you touch it? Make it a *crystal clear* image in your mind.

Read it every day. Add to it every day. Take advantage of this step.

Get emotionally involved with achieving it—get *excited*. Dreams come true doing this.

Create a plan. It could be the world's worst plan, but at least you can take action and learn. Without a plan, you're like a boat without a navigation chart. You have a destination but no chart to follow. There is no waypoint to direct your energy towards, and you'll likely end up on the rocks.

Retrain your subconscious mind to accept that you can do precisely what you want and that fear is not an option. If you experience fear in the form of anxiety, you can rest assured that you are about to grow. Moving past the anxiety and stepping into freedom is what growth is all about.

Align yourself with people that support you no matter how insane you think they think you are. You must do it yourself, but you can't do it alone. A business requires people; if you create a deep relationship with those people, you have no choice but to succeed.

Listen—nudity is a tool to use to be your authentic self. You don't have to be naked all the time to win in life, but having the attitude of a Naturist even when you have to wear clothes means you'll have more fun at driving your life instead of just eking out an existence.

Stop judging. When you judge others, you're criticizing. Ridiculing others, even in humour, is hurtful—especially self-deprecating humour. You're placing bad ideas in your subconscious mind that will stick like glue. Look at the world around you and see the wonder of it all. Be grateful, and the world will change for you. See the person, not the body or the clothing. Humans are genuinely good beings. Most need education, but all can love. Practice acceptance, tolerance, forgiveness, and love.

Love is something we can express as human beings. There are four types of love that we practice. We all know about erotic love—sexual attraction and the desire to experience an orgasm with someone. It's the shallowest form of the expression of love, but it's beautiful nonetheless. Then there's paternal love, the love that wants to nurture and guide others, especially offspring. Then there is brotherly love—when you love someone so much you'll do anything to help them. It's best described in a quote: "Yeah man! I love you, and I'll fight by your side 'til the end!"

But then there is Agape love (Pronounced, Ah-gah-pay). This is spiritual love. A love of all things and everyone. This is a real connection with Nature, and it is the best feeling you can imagine—unconditional, non-judgemental, peaceful love. Calmness overwhelms the body. When you learn to practice expressing Agape love, you will experience change within you that you may not currently believe possible. But when the realization falls upon you, you'll know it.

Reconnecting to Mother Earth on the physical plane, Nature on the spiritual plane, and, most importantly, to yourself and others on the intellectual plane—and finding balance on all three planes—will provide you with the most rewarding, healthy, and happy life imaginable.

Become a custodian of Mother Earth. Become selfless and help people, and you will succeed with speed.

Shed your clothes, sit beneath a tree, feel the breeze and sun all over, go skinny-dipping, have a cocktail with friends, and make a plan to succeed. Above all things, be authentic; speak the truth as you know it, while keeping an open mind to changing your ideas; love everything and everyone; and respond rather than react. Let your worries and doubts fester in the garbage, not in your mind. Relax and be free.

Naked, shameless, human, and free is all we want to be.

Printed in the United States
by Baker & Taylor Publisher Services